From Sandy Creek To Major League Fishing™

Manufactured in the United States of America

ISBN 978-0-692-21377-3

From Sandy Creek
To Major League
Fishing™

This book is my autobiography and it will detail my wonderful life and love of fishing. I have included many, many pictures of people who are part of my life, pictures of fishing and hunting events and the stories behind the pictures. This book will identify my favorite fishing places and baits I use to catch fish.

Dedication

Trish Konkler

I dedicate this book to all those I love dearly, especially to my wife of 44 years, Patricia "Trish" Jean Konkler. She is the most important person in my life. She is smart, dedicated, hardworking and loyal to the family. I am a better person because of her.

Dad, H.T., Mom, Dalton, Melton and Dorthell in front

To Mom, Elmer Rebecca "Becky" Konkler, for her moral guidance, love and care she gave me.

To Dad, Lewis Petter Konkler Jr., for the many fishing trips I took with him and his example of hard work and dedication to our family.

To my oldest brother, Melton Lewis Konkler, who was always my big brother even though he was short in stature.

Mom, Dad and Melton are deceased.

To my brother, Dalton Doyle Konkler, who I can call for advice about any mechanical machine and he knows what to do.

To my sister, Ola Dorthell Hurt, who is the hardest-working individual I know.

To my boys, Kristopher "Kris" Lewis Konkler and Heath "Bubba" Todd Konkler, who make me so proud and blessed to be their dad – they are very special.

To my daughter-in-law, Amber (Stallings) Konkler, who, every year, is mother-of-the-year to me. She homeschools our granddaughters, Rebekah Faith Konkler and Hope Allison Konkler, and gave me a grandson, Hank Titus Konkler.

To my nephew, Jeremy Shane Pittman, for his determination to succeed in life, and who is like a son to me.

To Stacie McFarlin, Kris' girlfriend, and her daughter, Ainsley McFarlin, who are family to me.

Amber, Rebekah, Heath, Hank and Hope in front

Kris and Stacie

Ainsley with Jimmy Huston at Bass Pro Shop

Jeremy, Salinda, Caleb and Abby

To my many uncles, aunts, cousins and mentors.

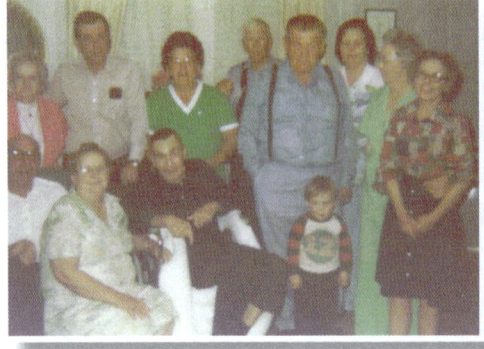

Konkler Aunts and Uncles:
Standing - Lucille, Tommy, Mom,
Dad, Ott, Juanita, Dot, Margie;
Seated - Clint, Ida, Bill and Kris
in front

Konkler Cousins at
Tommy and Margie
Bigham's 50th wedding
anniversary: Dwayne,
Andy, Dalton, H.T.,
Cecil, Lee and Don

Smith Cousins at 2009 Smith Family Reunion: Back - Harvey, Harley, H.T.,
David, Nathan, Jerry, Danny; Front - Deana, JoAnn, Ramona, Diane and Nova

Acknowledgment

I wrote this book at the suggestion of one of my favorite cousins, Ramona Hollan. We communicate a lot via email and have become great pen pals. She was a schoolteacher and wanted to write a book herself to give advice about what she

thinks makes a good teacher. Instead, she encouraged me to write this book. She even volunteered to proofread it for me. I value the judgment and dedication she gave me to get this book finished.

Ramona

Don and Marilyn

I also want to acknowledge my cousin, Don Lane, for giving me advice on writing a book, the cost involved and recommended publishers. I used the book Don wrote, *"What A Fantastic Life, The Life and Times of Donald C. Lane"* as a guide to write my book.

Grateful thanks is also given to Dave and Melanie King (http://kingstranscripts.wix.com/dmkings), who graciously walked us through the process of publication.

CONTENTS

Chapter   Page

1. Early Life (1944 – 1950) 11

2. Eldorado Grade School (1950 – 1956) 13

3. Eldorado Junior High (1957 – 1959) 14

4. Eldorado High School (1960 – 1962) 15

5. Eldorado Reunions 23

6. Dad - a Hard Working Man 25

7. Mom - My Moral Compass 28

8. Fishing Creeks and Ponds Around Eldorado 30

9. My Love of Hunting 35

10. Studying Pharmacy at Southwestern State College (1962 – 1965) ... 49

11. Fishing While in the Navy (1966 – 1969) 50

12. The Love of My Life 52

13. Studying Computer Science at OSU (1970 – 1972) 54

14. My Two Sons Kris and Heath (1974 and 1976) 55

15. Amoco Travels 57

16. Amoco Bass Club 58

17. Fishing the Annual Children's Tournament 63

18. Names of Bass Clubs and Major Tournaments I Have Fished 66

19. Fishing Bass Tournaments 67

20. Fishing in Old Mexico (1976 – 1986) 80

Chapter   Page

21. Fishing in Canada (2000 and 2002) 84

22. Fish Stories 85

23. My Favorite Lakes and Spots to Fish 101

24. My Favorite Baits to Catch Fish 101

25. Bass Pictures of Family and Friends 102

26. Catfish Pictures of Family and Friends 106

27. Crappie Pictures of Family and Friends 111

28. My Fish Recipe 122

29. Smith Family Reunion 122

30. Little Things in Life Make a Big Difference to Me 127

31. My Financial Advisor 132

32. Medical History 132

33. Basketball Official, Bowling and Other Happenings 133

34. Boat Official for Major League Fishing 141

35. And Finally 147

1
Early Life (1944 - 1950)

I was born on March 31, 1944, in Eldorado, OK. We lived in Bob and Mattie Taylor's home for one month then moved one block east to the house where I lived my school years in Eldorado. My sister, Dorthell, and her husband, Jerry Hurt, still maintain this house.

Eldorado is a small town with less than 500 people. My family lived on the east side of town with Uncle Sid Hall in the first house and us in the next house. Next were Barney (Eldorado barber), and Feeby Farley, Grandmother Evalena "Lena" Texana Smith, Mr. Shaw, and finally, Grandmother Maude Mae Konkler.

Smith Cousins: Back - Maxine, Sonny, Harley, Nathan; Middle - Marley, Alma, Cecil, Melton; Front - JoAnn, David, Mary, H.T. and Dalton

I was named after my grandfather, Henry Tildon Smith. I have only initials for a name. I named my second son, Heath Todd, using my initials and Heath named his son, Hank Titus, using my initials. In the Navy, they put (H) only (T) only for my name and some in the Navy called me Honly Tonly.

Grandfather and Grandmother Smith

I have three siblings. Melton is four years older than I am. Dalton, one year older and Dorthell is fourteen years younger.

When I was a baby, Dalton was still on the bottle. When mother gave both of us our bottles, he would drink all his milk, give me his empty bottle and drink the rest of my milk. He got big and I stayed small until about ninth grade. Eldorado folks called me, "PeeWee" and some of the folks still call me that today.

As a lad of five years, I pulled 200 pounds of cotton in one day and when I was 13, I pulled over 1,000 pounds. My coach, Roy Trammell Jr., gave me a silver dollar for pulling the 1,000 pounds. I still have that dollar today, 57 years later.

During my Eldorado school years, I chopped cotton (paid .75 cents/hr), pulled cotton (paid $2/hundred pounds), plowed (paid $1.25/hr) and mowed lawns (paid $2 to $3 per lawn). I also worked at the cotton gin sucking cotton out of trailers

H. T. Konkler, 5-year old son of Mr. and Mrs. Lewis Konkler empties his specially made tank in the nearly full cotton truck. Young Konkler stays right along with his parents in the field and can pull about 200 pound a day.

H.T. pulling 200 pounds of cotton in a day at 5 years old

(paid $1.25/hr), at the grain elevator unloading wheat trucks and removing wet sour wheat when water got into bins under the elevator (paid $1.25/hr). I also went on wheat harvest in the summer and worked at Toma's Grocery Store.

One time, when I was very young and while I was riding in the truck with Uncle Bud Wilson who was pulling a trailer load of cotton to the gin, he noticed a tire was rubbing against the wooden trailer and it was beginning to smoke. Consequently, we had to jump out of the truck to find some water to put on the fire, but there was no water. Uncle Bud began to pee on the trailer and so did I, but this little lad could not pee a stream big enough to solve the problem! Uncle Bud had told this story on me many times and we both laughed about it.

The first time I watched something on a TV set was at Mr. and Mrs. O.C. Wilson's place and we watched a boxing match. It was on a black and white screen. It was snowy and not very clear, but I was impressed anyway.

The first phones we had were the ones you crank the handle, get the local operator and then have her connect you to someone else in town who had a phone. Our phone number was 19. Sometimes you would pick up the phone and someone else would be talking because you were on a party line.

I remember Dad leaving the keys in the car or pickup at night. When we went on vacation, we never locked the house doors. I loved those vacations because Dad would stop at a cafe and buy five hamburgers for one dollar so we could get to eat more than one hamburger.

When we went to visit family in Sudan and Muleshoe, TX, we would stop at Bob's Oil Well Cafe in Matador, TX, and I got to see the live rattlesnakes that the owner kept inside the cafe. Outside the cafe was a big oil derrick as a landmark.

I remember Mom going to the washhouse in town to do our laundry and hanging the clothes on our clothesline just east of our house. She had a galvanized tub and scrub board if she needed to wash just a couple of things. The first washer and dryer Mom had was the one Trish and I bought her after we got married.

It seemed Mom could not keep dust off the furniture because we were always having a dust storm. You could see the dust coming from the west and it just came right through the windows. I also remember when visiting family in west Texas, we would drive through some of those dust storms and sometimes it was so bad that Dad would pull over to the side of the road because it was too dangerous to drive in the storm.

I remember being stung by ants, and Grandmother Konkler would put snuff on the sting spot. Grandmother dipped snuff. She used a stick with a knot on it

 to dip in her Garrett Snuff bottle and then put in her mouth. Her homemade remedy worked well.

*Grandfather and
Grandmother Konkler*

2
Eldorado Grade School (1950 – 1956)

My grade school teachers were Mrs. Holder in the first grade, Katherine Odom in the second grade, Madalene Slaton in the third grade and Lucille Wise in the fourth grade. In the fifth grade, we began to change classrooms. We had Roy Trammell, Mrs. Kincannon and Mrs. Hutchinson as teachers. We had the same teachers in the sixth grade as we had in the fifth grade. Mrs. Hutchinson's class was a big study hall room where fifth graders sat in the front of the room and sixth graders sat in the back of the room. Mrs. Hutchinson was our grade school principal.

Eldorado 5th Grade: Row 3 - Jerry Hamersley, Paula Brewer, Linda Easley, Linda Howard, Kay Hartley, Sandy Hulett, Jolene Rice, Darrell Jones, Wendell Doughten, James Gilley, Melvin Springer;   Row 2 - Dalton Konkler, Joe Stroud, Paul McHendry, Jerry Mitchell, H.T. Konkler, Wayne Nix, Roger Skinner, Le Roy Hooker, Freddy Floyd;   Row 1 - Betty Reeves, Susie Cleverdon, Cheryl Littlefield, Lynda Bernard, JoAnn Mitchell, Carol Barker, Janette Weddle and Linda Hale

I was around eight years old when we got our first bathroom in the house. We used a two-seat outhouse until then. I remember using catalogs for toilet paper. Before we got the bathroom, I took baths in a galvanized tub, generally on a Saturday evening.

The first vehicle I drove was a jeep owned by my Uncle Ralph Konkler. I was nine or ten years old. Uncle Ralph lived with Grandmother Konkler four houses north of us. One day, he stopped by our house and asked me to drive while he held a rope tied to a cow that he was taking home. The jeep was a stick shift, and when I let out the clutch, I pushed the gas pedal too fast that nearly jerked my uncle out of the vehicle.

It seems if we got sick castor oil was the medicine we would take, but I also remember getting sick in grade school and Mom made me stay home and gave me a Dr Pepper to drink. I think those Cokes and Dr Peppers in small bottles tasted so much better then than they do today.

The first wheat harvest I made was when I was seven or eight years old. Dad went on wheat harvest with the Hamersley brothers. I remember traveling with Mom and Mrs. Hamersley to Kansas where the men were cutting wheat. I

Jerry Hamersley

remember playing under one of the wheat trucks, raising up and splitting my head open when I hit the steel beam under the truck. I do not remember how many stitches it took, but I do remember bleeding a lot.

Speaking of the Hamersleys, the hardest I have ever been hit by a person was by Jerry Lee Hamersley in the fourth grade. I do not even remember why he hit me, but I do remember the hit.

I remember going to the Ritz Theater owned by the Cleverdons to watch movies like Roy Rogers, Gene Autry and Jack the Ripper. I still remember how scared I was walking home the night I watched Jack the Ripper.

3
Eldorado Junior High (1957 – 1959)

These were my teachers at junior high, and the subjects they taught us:

- C.G. McMindes – Agriculture
- Denise Stroud – Home Economics
- Roy Trammell – Physical Education and History
- Lou Helen White – Music and English
- Marjorie Dial – Math
- Noble McKibbons – Math and History

I did not get many spankings in school, but if I did, I knew I would also get one at home from Dad. I remember one spanking was from coach Trammel when I was in junior high. We played a basketball game at Victory and when the girls were the ones playing, some of us boys went outside popping firecrackers and Coach found out about it. The next day at practice, he lined up the team and gave each one a hit with a paddle that we made him in shop class. It was a good paddle. It had holes that we drilled in and could swing really well to get a maximum effect.

H.T. at 9 years old

H.T. at 10 years old

H.T. at 8 years old

4
Eldorado High School (1960 – 1962)

Following were my high school teachers, and the subjects they taught:

- C.G. McMindes – Agriculture
- Denise Stroud – Home Economics
- Roy Trammell – Physical Education, Civics, and Oklahoma History
- Melvin Richeson - English
- Bob Durham - Biology
- Dale Culver – General Science and Math
- Mrs. Culver – English, Literature, and Typing

My junior high and high school principal was Don Henry, and my superintendent was Bob Durham. I liked all my teachers, principals and superintendents, but I had favorites whom I proudly called my mentors.

Mrs. Slaton taught us in grade school, and even after I got married and had children, she not only remembered me, she also remembered my boys.

Mrs. White, my Music teacher, loved us, even though some of us could not carry a tune in a bucket. She always had a smile on her face. She was also my English teacher and she taught me when to use 'a' vs. 'an', 'here' vs. 'hear' and other appropriate words. She let our class swim in her pond southwest of town when we were in high school. That was fun, but it was muddy water and we looked terrible. We had to go to another pond that was clear so we could clean up.

Coach Trammel was someone I always loved to talk with when I returned to Eldorado to visit. I was so honored to be a pallbearer when we laid him to rest.

Mr. McMinds was our Agriculture teacher and I probably learned more about life in his class than any class I have attended. We had a lot of projects and made many things for the community. We went on many field trips and learned how to work with livestock and do other farming chores. He had us borrow $100 from our banker, George Littlefield. Not because we needed it, but to learn that we must pay back what we borrow.

Mrs. Stroud taught us manners and the proper way to act when at the dinner table. I spent many days at her house, because her son, Joe and I were classmates and great friends. I am not going to list all the mischief that Joe and I did.

My favorite swimming holes were on John A. Richardson's farm on Sandy Creek and Junior Gunkel pond east of town.

A friend, Gary Babb, was at our house and we were playing and hiding from each other. He ran into the bathroom and hid. We have a hall next to the bathroom where our guns are stored so I picked up a 22 pump and pointed it at the bathroom door and told Gary if he did not come out I would pull the trigger. We did not keep our guns loaded, but one shell had stuck in the chamber and when I pumped the gun and pulled the trigger, the gun went off. Luckily, Gary was not sitting on the toilet seat because the bullet went through the door and hit the toilet lid. Did I get a spanking from Dad for this stupid act? Well, what do you think?

Mom took Dalton and I to Joe Williams hog farm northwest of town to pick some plums for Mom to make plum jelly and plum butter, my favorite. Dalton and I had picked about two bushels of plums but Dalton did not want to carry them back to the barn where Mom dropped us off. Instead, he went to the barn where Joe had a tractor parked. Dalton figured out he needed to hand crank the tractor to start it. He got it started, drove it to the plum thicket, picked up our plums, carried them to the barn and then parked the tractor where he found it leaving the tractor low on water. About a week later, Joe found out the water pump was bad and talked to Dad about it. Dad had to pay Joe for the repair and Dalton and I paid our part, but it was not with money.

We had a family dog named Spot, the first dog I remember that lived until I was 14 years old. One time after that when Mom and Dad traveled to western Texas to visit with Uncle Bud and Aunt Lavern, I got to go hunting for jackrabbits where Uncle Bud worked in the oil fields. Imagine me hunting with a .22 rifle in an oil field. Before we left for Eldorado, I noticed the neighbors had a litter of bird dogs. I stole one of the puppies, put it in Dad's car and hid it under a blanket in the back seat. They did not notice the puppy until we got to Eldorado. Mom called Aunt Lavern, and her neighbors said it was okay for me to keep the dog.

But I believe God had punished me for stealing the dog. About a week after we were home, Dalton was sleeping on the porch in a fold-up bed and it began to rain. He hurriedly folded up the bed and came inside. The next day, I was looking for my puppy and did not find it until I looked in the fold-up bed and there it was. Yep, the puppy was a goner! This was my punishment for stealing something.

One of my pets when I was young was a skunk. Dad knew how to de-scent skunks. Once, he captured some baby skunks from under a house, brought one home and fixed it so it would not stink. That cat roamed all throughout our home and never smelled like a skunk.

In the summer time, we put a bed between our house and the washhouse. I would put a cloth screen mesh over the bed so mosquitoes would not bother us. It was great for sleeping with the breeze blowing between the house and the washhouse protecting us from the sun in the early hours of the morning.

When it rained around Eldorado, some dirt roads would be so muddy that it was hard to drive a vehicle on them. I must have been around 11 or 12 years old when Dad and Mom visited Uncle Bill and Aunt Ida about 10 miles north of Eldorado. It began to rain very hard and by the time we started back to Eldorado, the dirt roads were extremely muddy. Dad had a 1959 green Chevrolet with fender skirts and mud would cake around

H.T. holding bobcat by our washhouse

the wheels making it hard to move. Melton, Dalton and I pushed the car for miles in the mud. Needless to say, Mom had some muddy clothes to wash by the time we got to Eldorado.

I always liked the time around the 4th of July when some of my cousins, for example, Lee Allen and Dwayne Lane and Gene and Gerald Konkler, would visit and we would pop firecrackers. We would buy some cherry bomb firecrackers and place them under tin cans to see how far it would blow the can in the air.

One of our favorite things to do in Eldorado was to play pool at Bill Leese Pool Hall or Shorty Davis Pool Hall. We played regular pool, 8-ball pool and snooker. Bill Leese Pool Hall had tables in the back for people to play dominoes, forty-two, moon or pitch and Shorty Davis was known to sell some moonshine sometimes.

Once in a while a group of us would get rambunctious like that one night when we decided to steal watermelons from Pup Hankins' farm west of town. Ricky, Joe, Bobby, Jerry, Dalton and I were in his watermelon patch and Pup knew we were there. He called Bill Berge, our town sheriff, and they scared the daylights out of us! Bill shot a shotgun with rock salt over our heads and we started running back to our two pickups parked on the road. It was a half-mile run. When we got to the fence, only Dalton had watermelons. He had one under each arm.

One evening after plowing the fields of Pill Hulett, and I was coming home, I spotted a big rattlesnake crossing the road. I backed up in my pickup slowly to look in the ditch to try locating the snake, and on driving forward, I noticed that

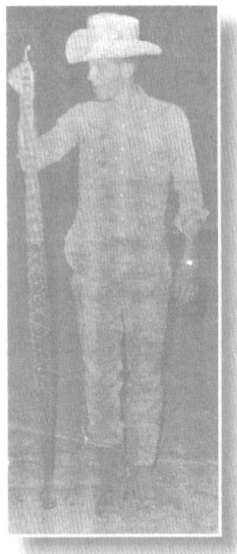

the snake was just across the barbed wire fence coiled in a striking position. I got out of the truck, found a big rock and tossed it at the snake. The rock just bounced off its back and made the snake mad; then I found a fence post, crossed the fence and began to pound the snake on the head.

Later on, Ricky and I played a trick on Tom Pearsy, a farmhand for the Huletts, with this big rattlesnake I killed. I brought the snake to the farm and coiled it on the gearshift of Tom's tractor. That morning as he started to climb on his tractor, he got startled by the snake. He hurriedly jumped off and swiftly ran away. Ricky and I were laughing so hard knowing that the snake was dead. After Tom figured out what was happening he started chasing us.

H.T. with rattlesnake killed when plowing for Pill Hulett

I went on wheat harvest with Pete and Clem Terry. I worked for Clem while Joe Stroud, a classmate, and Joe Harkins, a schoolmate, worked for Pete. We cut wheat in Eldorado and moved north as the wheat ripened in the northern states, for example, Kansas and Nebraska. I sometimes drove the combine with a 12-foot header. Other times, I would drive the truck to haul the wheat to the elevator.

Once when driving the truck to town, I ran over a pheasant. I stopped and picked it up and brought it to where we were staying. I cleaned the pheasant and Mrs. Terry cooked it for me.

One summer when we returned from Kansas, Gerald Neely, a schoolmate, was in Eldorado taking a safety class for bus driving. He asked me to go with him to Nebraska to finish cutting some wheat his dad was cutting. I spent a week with them cutting wheat.

Another summer, I plowed land east of Eldorado for District Judge Weldon Ferris. My cousin, David Beckett, and his family were visiting us. One day, David went to the field with me and while we rode on the WD-9 tractor pulling a one-way plow, suddenly the tractor sped up. I looked at the plow and half of it was missing. I had to call the judge and had him come out and help us.

The WD-9 tractor ran on propane, and one day while filling the tank on the tractor, I noticed a rattlesnake next to where I was working. I sprayed the snake with the propane and it froze the snake.

One thing I remember about the judge was that when he picked me up in his red and white Fairlane Ford car, he had a box of King Edward cigars in the front seat. It seemed he always had a cigar hanging out of his mouth.

I also remember the judge fining me and my now brother-in-law, Gary Huckabay, for hunting dove without our hunting licenses. This was in fall of 1962 on a Sunday and Gary and I were heading to Weatherford, OK, to start our first day of college at Southwestern State College. We decided to drive around and hunt dove before we left for college. Normally, I would buy my hunting and fishing license each fall but forgot to do it that year. There were several game wardens patrolling the area both in the air and on land. They spotted Gary and me hunting so they stopped and checked us for our licenses. I cannot remember how much we paid, but the judge did fine us and scolded us for not being responsible.

From my junior year in high school and through some of my college years, I worked for Frank Toma at his grocery store. I loved the end of the week when Frank would take some steaks home and invite me to dinner. Nita, his wife, would cook the steaks, fry some potatoes and make biscuits and gravy. Sometimes during the week after work, Frank would take a couple of t-bone steaks to the Panther Drive-In, which was operated and owned by Eula Williams, my future mother-in-law and she would cook them for us.

During the fall, we had cotton-harvest people come to town, and Frank would stay open seven days a week and long hours each day. Eldorado School would not be open during cotton harvest time so kids could help harvest the crops. I opened the store each morning and stayed until we closed the store. I remember working 105 hours one week.

Not only did Frank feed me well, he also loaned me his 1955 Chevrolet to travel to college at Southwestern State College at Weatherford, OK, where I was studying to be a pharmacist. It was 230 miles round trip. I would come home on the weekends and work in his store.

Frank would let people charge groceries and pay for them later. My folks did that and I found out they had an old bill and owed over $500. I decided that I would pay their bill and I paid a little each week until I got the bill paid. I believe that is one reason Frank was so kind to me. He knew I was competent and trustworthy.

Frank, his son, Paul and I fished many ponds around Eldorado, mostly trying to catch catfish. Hugo Hartley's pond was our favorite and we would fish the pond at night after we closed the store. We would bring the catfish we caught to the store and clean them on the chopping block. Frank and I also built places for the catfish to lay their eggs during spawning time. We took old wooden crates from his store that we received groceries in and made spawning huts by putting legs on the boxes and cutting holes for the catfish to get inside the dark area. We waded into Hugo's pond and pushed the boxes into the mud so they would stay in one position.

Frank and I fished the Early Freeman pond east of Eldorado when there were many, many small catfish, two to six inches. We would put the small catfish in

H.T., Paul, Dalton, Frank - cleaning catfish, and Dorthell

a barrel full of water and place a burlap sack over the top to keep the water from sloshing out when we transferred the small catfish to other ponds to stock them with catfish. Our favorite pond to stock was the Cavener pond north of town. It was small, had many red-horse minnows and plenty of crawdads. Many times, we stopped at the Cavener pond to seine minnows and crawdads and used to catch bass and catfish on the Robinson pond about a mile north of the Cavener pond. We also used old meat from Frank's grocery store as bait to catch catfish. The biggest one we caught from the Robinson pond was around eight pounds. Because the Cavener pond had so much bait in the pond we stocked it heavily with the small catfish.

One year later, we took some fishing poles to the pond and caught some catfish. It was unbelievable! The catfish were already in the 1.5 pounds to three pounds weights. Well, that didn't last very long because some of the local folks in Eldorado found out about the catfish and went out one night and spread rotenone (generally used as a fisheries management chemical) on the water and killed all the fish and bait in the Cavener pond. I later learned they picked up all the fish and cleaned them for a fish fry. Frank and I were not pleased to say the least. We also stocked the Polk Crozier pond northwest of town and a couple of more ponds but never caught good fish from them as we did the Cavener pond.

Frank always had a lot of money in his pocket. He carried a roll of bills and many times paid for things in cash. I saw Frank pull out enough cash from his pocket to pay for a new car. He also saved money at his house in a wooden box that he had the top nailed shut. He had a slit in the top of the box where he put $5, $10 and $20 dollar bills. He also put half dollars and silver dollars in the box. He counted the money once and there was over $10,000. Whenever Frank took checks to the bank to have them deposited or cashed, he left me in charge of the store.

Frank loved to play dominoes, and many times, he would stop at Bill's Pool Hall and play dominoes. Frank allowed me to pay the bread, milk and other vendors. I either paid cash or paid with a check that Frank had already signed.

I did everything in that store. I cut meat, stocked the shelves, swept the floor, checked out customers and carried their groceries to their vehicle. I even learned a little of Spanish from Jesse Ramos, one of our customers.

Eldorado High School Baseball Team: Standing - H.T., Gerald, Jerry, Coach Trammell, Melvin, Darrell; Kneeling - Boyd, Ricky, Gary, Bruce, George, Bobby and Joe

One summer when I sold Bibles in Lebanon OH, I was on my way home to Eldorado at the end of summer, and Nita Toma wanted to surprise me with a party. She planned the party, invited my friends and prepared the food. The only problem was that I was late to the party by one day. Everyone I talked to said they really enjoyed my party even though I was not there.

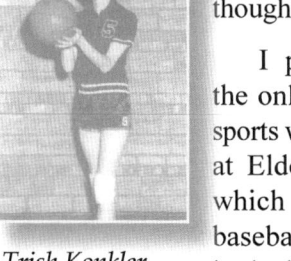

Trish Konkler

I played the only two sports we had at Eldorado, which were baseball and basketball. I was fortunate to have Coach Trammel as my grade school, junior high school and high school coach, both in baseball and basketball.

Eldorado High School Basketball Team: Standing - Darrell, Melvin, Coach Trammell, H.T., Gerald; Kneeling - Bruce, Boyd, Jim, Ricky, Bobby and Al

I graduated from Eldorado High School in 1962. There were 23 in my class when I graduated and they were:

- Paula Brewer – "Best Dancer"
- Betty Wilson Braker – Transfer Student
- Levena Meeks Easley – "Most Scholarly"
- Kay Hartley – "Most Talented"
- Gary Huckabay – "Most Scholarly"
- Rita James - "Most Promising Future"
- Sandy Hulett – "Best Dressed"
- Darrell Jones – "Best Athlete"
- H. T. Konkler – "Most Promising Future"
- Cheryl Littlefield – "Cutest"
- Jacquita Mefford – "Best Athlete"
- Jerry Mitchell – "Best Dressed"
- Jo Ann Mitchell – "Most Beautiful"
- Tommie Pruitt – Transfer Student
- Betty Reeves
- Jolene Rice – "Best All Around"
- Lynda Bernard Sherwood – "Most Popular"
- Kenneth Springer – "Most Handsome"
- Melvin Springer – "Wittiest"
- Calva Story – "Most of the Best"
- Joe Stroud – "Best Dancer"
- Earl Taylor – "Biggest Wolf"
- Janette Weddle – "Biggest Flirt"

In our early years at Eldorado, we had as many as 33 in our class. Some of those who moved away before they graduated still visit when we have a reunion.

Eldorado 1962 Graduation Class

5
Eldorado Reunions

Beginning in 1961, we began to have a reunion for everyone who graduated from Eldorado. The first reunion was in 1961 and then we had a reunion every five years starting in 1965.

Eldorado Reunion in 1985 (Class of 1962). Back Row - Betty, Janette, H.T., Gary, Kay; Front Row - Rita, JoAnn, Paula, Jaquita and Susie

Eldorado Reunion in 1995 (Class of 1962). Back Row - Joe, Sandy, Rita, Trish, Jaquita, Jolene, JoAnn; Front - H.T., Kathy and Betty

Eldorado Reunion in 2000: H.T. and Trish

I graduated from Eldorado in 1962, and our class had a 40th reunion in 2002 and a 45th reunion in 2007. Our latest get-together was in Oklahoma City on Memorial Day, 2013. Eight of us (Cheryl, Darrell, Emilee, JoAnn, Paula, Rita, Wayne and I) met. We had lunch together, reminisced about the past and

brought each other up-to-date on what was going on in our lives. We definitely are looking forward to another get together.

Eldorado Reunion in 2002 (40th year): Roger, Janette, Jaquita, Paula, Wayne, Jerry, Susie, Betty, H.T., Rita, Linda, Sandy, JoAnn and Darrell

Above: Eldorado Reunion in 2007 (45th year): Back Row - Cheryl, Roger, Darrell, Jerry, Lynda, H.T., Janette; Front Row - Susie, Sandy, Kay, JoAnn, Paula, Calva, Betty, Rita and Jaquita

Eldorado Class of 1962 on Memorial Day 2013: Kay, Wayne, Cheryl, Darrell, Paula, Rita, JoAnn and H.T.

6
Dad, A Hard Working Man

Dad generally kept a cow, chickens and hogs. Part of my chores was to take care of them.

Dad would go to work at the Quanah Cotton Seed Oil Mill, then meet us in the cotton field and pull cotton until dark. Mom made our lunch to take to the cotton fields and it generally contained pork chops, pork and beans and cold tea. The night before we headed to the cotton field, I would put a quart of tea in the freezer and let it thaw out the next day while we were pulling cotton.

Mom and Dad

Mom and Dad

My first fishing days were on Sandy Creek. Dad loved to fish Sandy Creek using a cane pole with 75 pounds test braided line, a pencil shaped cork and stink bait. Dad would take me with him to fish for catfish. Dad generally bought stink bait from the Schotts family in Quanah, TX, where he worked. The bait was made from minnows, which were seined from Red River and put on a tin roof to dry, then they were ground in a meat grinder with ingredients added, generally, sweet anise oil.

Dad and Dorthell

In the summer when I was not in school, Dad would drop me off on Sandy Creek on his way to work at Quanah. I would have a cane pole, a bag with extra hooks, weights and corks, and I generally fished a couple of miles of the creek then walked back home, which was a mile or two. All the people in Eldorado knew me so if I

Dad and Jeremy

was walking home from the creek, someone generally stopped and gave me a ride home. Sometimes I would walk the train tracks back to town. The tracks were a block south of our house. The tracks ran through the middle of town so they were a block from everyone's house.

Stink bait was my favorite bait for catfish, but worms were my favorite if I was trying to catch anything that would bite. I watered some soil in the cow lot east of the house and kept a piece of wood over the wet dirt so it would draw worms to the area. I could depend on finding worms there when I needed them. I also used grasshoppers, chicken liver, blood bait made from chicken blood, fishing shrimp, minnows both live and dead, crawdads, perch, shad, frogs, Limburger cheese mixed with calf brains, whole kernel corn and a concoction like mashed wheaties with strawberry soda.

Dad maintained about 10 beehives and we had plenty of honey to eat. Dad had an extractor that we put the frames of honey in and extracted the honey. We would put honey in quart and pint jars, some with and some without wax in the honey. The honey wax you could chew just like gum. Dad sold some of the honey at $1 for a pint and $1.75 for a quart. I got stung many times by the bees and sometimes I would go to school with a swollen lip or a shut eye.

In the summer when the queen bee lay her eggs sometimes she would lay another queen bee and when that happened the new queen would leave the hive with some drone and worker bees and create a swarm generally on some tree branch. We would capture the new swarm in a beehive. Drone bees took care of the queen and worker bees would bring pollen back to the hive to make honey.

Dad did not go to church. He would tell Mom, "You only need to go to church when you are bad." However, when Melton was killed that changed for Dad.

One Saturday night when I was working in Toma's Grocery Store, Dad came in and asked me what I was doing Sunday morning. I thought he wanted to go

fishing so I told him I was not doing anything. He asked if I would go to the Baptist Church with him. I was surprised but very happy he wanted to go to church. That morning he went to the altar and asked God to forgive him of his sins. I went to the altar and prayed with Dad. That is one moment I will never forget!

2013 Smith Reunion dominoe game: Dalton, Jap, Lee and Jake

Our family loved to play dominoes. Mom had one brother (Lucian Smith) and five sisters (Opal Hadley, Marie Beckett, Jewel Rich, Mattie Price, and Lavern Wilson). Dad had three brothers (Johnny Konkler, Doyle Konkler, and Ralph Konkler) and five sisters (Dot Lee, Lucile Lane, Ida Bryant, Margie Bigham, and Josephine Ewing) and most of them played dominoes. After the adults finished playing dominoes, my cousins and I would play dominoes. That is where I learned to love math. I enjoyed counting.

Dad's oldest sister was named Dot. Because Aunt Dot and Uncle Ott (his real name was Otis) did not have children, she would buy each of her nephews and nieces a gift for Christmas. I remember getting a wallet from her for Christmas and it would always contain money. Aunt

Dalton, H.T. and Heath playing dominoes

Dot and Uncle Ott loved to fish especially on Fort Gibson. They kept a small aluminum boat in a boathouse in Toppers. Aunt Dot liked to fish for sand bass and Uncle Ott liked to fish for catfish. When I was young, they took me fishing with them. Before we would go to the lake, Uncle Ott would take me to some catalpa trees and we would pick catalpa worms from the leaves for catfish bait.

In 1976 when Heath was born, Mom was in Tulsa helping with the newborn baby, and we got a call that Dad was in an accident at the Quanah Cotton Seed Oil Mill, where he worked. Dad was a foreman and he was checking to see why the floor auger was not running in the building where the cottonseed was stored. He noticed seeds were clogged, so he crawled down into the area and began to unclog the seed. A co-worker did not realize that Dad was working on the problem and hit the start button on the auger. It grabbed Dad's leg and cut it off just below the knee. Since then Dad used a prosthesis leg the rest of his life.

When Dad and I would go fishing on Sandy Creek and we had a fence to cross, he would take off the prosthesis leg. He would toss it over the fence then pull himself over the fence, fall on the ground and put his prosthesis leg back on. We would then try to catch a catfish.

When Dad and Mom were visiting Trish and me in Tulsa, I took them fishing on Oologah. We put my boat in at a place that was not really a ramp, but instead off the side of the road where it ended in Lighting Creek. We had no problem unloading the boat and pulling out the trailer. However, when we were ready to leave I tried to pull the trailer out with the boat on it and my pickup tires would

just spin. Luckily, another angler was there. He tied to my pickup and the both of us got the boat and trailer out onto the road.

Another thing happened while we were in the creek. I was turning into an arm of the creek and had to go over a log and when I did, it bent the steering cable to the motor. I could still drive the boat, but it was hard to steer. Later I had to have the steering cable replaced. We caught a few bass and crappie that day, but I think Dad and Mom were thinking "Didn't we teach our son any common sense?"

Another time when Dad and Mom came to Tulsa to visit, Dad and I went fishing for bass on Eufaula. When Dad got into the boat, he sat in the back pedestal seat. Because he had a prosthesis leg, I tried to get him to move down and sit in the seat next to me, but he wanted to stay in that seat and he did, even when I was running in the back of Duchess Creek. He also stayed there when we were fishing. He got in the seat that morning and stayed there until we were ready to come home.

I lost Dad to a very long illness in November of 1984. Dad was a humble man and what I remember most was that he worked hard and took time to help others, never expecting anything in return.

7
Mom, My Moral Compass

Mom

M om took me to the Pentecostal Holiness Church when I was young, but when I got in high school, I

started going to church at the Baptist Church because some of my high school classmates were going there. Mom went to church every time the door was open. As a matter of fact, she had a key to the church. I

Dad and Mom

remember walking by our bathroom and hearing Mom praying. She said many prayers in that bathroom. I never heard Mom say a curse word or anything bad about anyone. She always saw the good in people.

Mom always cooked breakfast, lunch and supper (yep, we call it supper instead of dinner) and most times she would cook more than one meat for each meal. We always had fresh meat, eggs, milk, butter, jelly and honey to eat. If Mom wanted to cook chicken, she would have me catch a chicken from the yard, wring its neck, scald it in hot water and pluck its feathers. She would cut it up and cook it. We raised pigs that we showed at the Jackson County Fair in Altus, OK. If the pig did not make the auction, then Dad would butcher it, sugar cure the meat and hang the meat in the washhouse. If she wanted to cook pork, we would retrieve meat from the washhouse. I loved that sugar cured ham and fresh bacon. Dad also had other hogs and it was my job to give the hogs their slop. We did not have a garbage disposal, but instead saved the food scraps (slop) and fed that to the hogs. We ate plenty of fresh fish because of the fish that we caught in the creeks and ponds. I gathered a lot of eggs from the shed just east of our house and milked a cow in the same shed. Sometimes there would be a cat in the shed while I was milking the cow and I would squirt the cat in the mouth with milk, which the cat liked. I loved the fresh milk but I did not like buttermilk, which we got when we churned the skimmed cream. I sat at that churn many times with a wooden broom-like pole churning up and down until there was butter. I made fun of my cousins who lived in the 'big' city of Tulsa because they drank homogenized milk purchased at the store and would not drink the fresh milk.

We generally ate plum jelly or plum butter from the plums we gathered from plum bushes on local farmers land. Mom also had an apricot tree in the garden and made apricot jelly. Mom's fried apricot pies, about the size of a taco, were delicious.

H.T. and his pig for Eldorado 4H

When I milked our cow, I did not use a milking machine like most dairy farmers do today. I tied the cow to a post, fed her some food, sat on a small stool, put my head in the cow's crouch and pulled on those tits. The reason for putting my head in her crouch is that generally there were flies in the barn when I milked her and she would try to swat those flies with her tail when they landed on her. That tail would hurt if she hit me with it. Sometimes the cow would either kick or just lift her leg and I had to pull the milk bucket out of the way, so she would not spill my bucket of milk. There were several times I went back to the house with less milk than I should have.

Dad had a big garden and he planted tomatoes, onions, cucumbers, okra, beans, peas, squash, beets and potatoes.

One of my favorite foods was cornbread and beans. Mom would fix pinto beans, navy beans, or butterbeans. Dad loved to eat chow-chow (made from green tomatoes) with his pinto beans.

Mom would let me help cook, especially if it was biscuits. I would mix flour, milk, baking powder and a pinch of salt. If I wanted the biscuits to rise more, I would add more baking powder. I would roll the dough out on a board and cut biscuits out using a drinking glass.

There was a cellar just outside our back door and Mom used it to store food that she canned. She canned plums, beans, peas, okra, tomatoes, pickles and peaches, and put the jars on the shelves in the cellar. There was a kerosene lamp, cot beds and a couple of chairs in the cellar. It seemed Mom took us to the cellar every time a dark cloud appeared. But not Dad! He only came to the cellar when a storm was really, really bad.

I lost Mom to cancer in October of 1996. One story about Mom, she had great respect for those in the military. One person in Eldorado who was in the Army during the Vietnam War told me that he received $5 a month from Mom while he was in the service. I found out that Mom gave money to others in the military, from Eldorado. Mom did not have much money, but she gave to military folks and paid her tithes in church.

8
Fishing Creeks and Ponds Around Eldorado

One time when I was in the fourth or fifth grade, I came home from school and no one was home, so I grabbed my cane pole and headed to Sandy Creek Bridge between Eldorado and Quanah. The reason no one was home was because Uncle Arnold and Aunt Marie were visiting and they had gone somewhere with Mom and Dad. When they got home, Mom and Dad were concerned that I was not home and assumed I went fishing. Dad and Uncle Arnold drove to the creek bridge hoping I would be there and thank goodness, I was there. Normally this would have been one of those times I would get a spanking (yes, I got more than one), but since we had company, Dad took it easy on me and just scolded me, telling me how it scared him and Mom. I was thankful I did not get a spanking and proud because I caught one catfish that weighed 2.5 pounds that we brought home and cleaned.

Sometimes I would ride my bicycle, with my cane pole tied to it, to the creek and fish from daylight to noon, then come home. I fished Sandy Creek from the Spradlin farm all the way to the mouth of Sandy Creek that flows into Red River, which is about 15 to 20 miles of creek. The deepest hole in the creek was at the mouth and was over my head in depth. One time Jimmy Tinsley, my brother-in-law, and a friend, Keith Hooper, and I took a flat-bottomed boat, dumped into the creek at the mouth and set out some bank poles. One of the main reasons we always had fish in Sandy Creek was because when the Red River got high, it would bring fish upstream and they would come into the creeks. Many fish and bait were hatched in Sandy Creek because it always contained water coming from the many springs in the creek. One place on the upper end of Jake Stroud's farm on Sandy Creek was named Seven Springs because it had that many springs in one area. In the summer, those springs felt good when we waded through them.

Many of my cousins, for example, Andy and Bill Bigham, David Beckett, Danny Wilson, and others loved to go with my brothers and me to fish Sandy Creek. Most of the time it was a great experience, but one time when we waded the creek and set out some bank poles, the creek was high and water was flowing fast.

Andy and Tommy with catfish from Sandy Creek

David was visiting then and went with us to the creek. In water that was not deep, there was no problem for David, but in water over our heads, David had to get on Dalton's back. Dalton's mistake was to let David do that, because David kept pushing Dalton under water and Dalton thought he was going to drown. Luckily, there were plenty of low hanging tree branches that Dalton could grab that kept him above water with David on his back. We decided it was safer for our David just to walk the bank when the water was deep.

When I took my cousins fishing on Sandy Creek we would wade the creek and check the poles at night. We had good flashlights. If you shine a flashlight on a snake, it will swim right

H.T. and Andy with catfish from Sandy Creek

up to you. I did this on several different trips and then turned out the light. My cousins would run like crazy in the water. Sometimes we took a machete knife with us and we would whack the snake when it got close to us. We called the snakes, water moccasins, but actually, they were just water snakes. The water moccasin or cottonmouth is a highly venomous snake. Of all my trips fishing Sandy and Boggy Creeks I have only seen one water moccasin and that was with Dad on Jake Stroud's place on Sandy Creek. We also used the flashlight to blind frogs on the bank so we could grab them. They made good catfish bait.

Dad would take Aunt Marie, Aunt Jewel, Aunt Lavern, Mom, and sometimes me to Sandy Creek, generally on the Henderson land south of town to fish for catfish. We could always tell when Aunt Marie would catch a fish because she would holler really loud and anyone within a mile of her could hear her.

The Henderson land was a favorite part of Sandy Creek that Dad liked to fish. To fish that part of the creek we had to go through a gate by Harrison Cox's house. Harrison was a bachelor and not always a pleasant person to be around. Occasionally Dad would take a six-pack of beer and give it to Harrison, which I believe is one reason that Harrison always liked Dad and me.

Another person who took me fishing was Mr. Shaw who loved to fish for perch and mudcats or anything that would bite. Grandmother Konkler would fry those fish for us and I ate many times with her and Mr. Shaw.

Ida "Red" Kelly took me fishing with her also. The nickname Red came from her bright red hair. I would go to her house early in the morning and she would fix me hot tea. The first and only hot tea I ever drank. I love cold unsweetened tea and drink plenty of it today.

Paul, Heath, Kris, Jeremy and H.T. with bass caught in Fred Goss pond

My brothers and I would catch carp in Sandy Creek by taking a 15 to 20-foot seine and circle overhanging trees, brush on the bank of the creek, stick each pole into the bank, then get inside the seine and catch the carp with our hands. We would put them in a burlap sack and Dad would take them to work and give to the coworkers, who loved to eat them.

Fred Goss, who lived in Eldorado, also liked to eat carp and I would take some by his place. He was always grateful and let me fish on his pond south of town by the cemetery. I caught many bass in that pond.

I fished many ponds around Eldorado and that is where I began my love for catching bass. I caught most of them on a lure called a Shyster. Most were either white with black spots or yellow with black spots, had a blade that spun around the wire and a treble hook on the end with tail feathers. I used other baits, but this was my favorite for catching bass. I fished with a Zebco rod and reel (a 33 reel, which in my option was the best reel that Zebco made at that time).

Later in life, I came back to Eldorado and fished these ponds with spinnerbaits, buzzbaits, plastic worms and other baits. I caught many bass on these baits.

I first learned about spawning bass on the Ore Smith pond northeast of town. Some cedar trees were partly underwater on the dirt dam and bass would spawn around these trees. This is where I learned how bass react to different baits, while on the bed.

I fished Lugert Lake, north of Altus, OK and Pauline Lake, east of Quanah, TX. Most of the time, I was fishing for anything. If I were trying to catch a bass or crappie, I would use live minnows, if I was trying to catch catfish, I would use stink bait, dead minnows, or worms, and if I were trying to catch carp, I would use dough bait. My favorite bait for carp was wheaties mashed and strawberry pop added to make dough balls. Another carp bait was made from cottonseed meal, mixed with sugar and water, then cooked and made into dough balls.

My brothers and I seined minnows, small perch and crawdads in Sandy Creek to use as bait on our bank poles. Melton and I seemed to enjoy the fishing more than Dalton. My cousin, Eugene Taylor, often went with me to set out bank poles. A.G. Taylor, Eugene's Dad, loved to fish Boggy Creek, so sometimes Eugene and I would put our bank poles out on Boggy Creek. Sandy Creek was much bigger than Boggy Creek and it contained more fish, so most of the time we fished Sandy Creek.

A bank pole most often was a willow pole that was four to six feet long, with all the branches trimmed and a line with lead weight and hook attached to the pole. We sometimes used a cedar pole, but not very often because the cedar pole did not float, but willow poles did float. Sometimes a catfish would pull the pole out of the bank and when they did, we would search the creek for the butt end of the bank pole that was sticking up. We waded Sandy Creek and stuck poles in the bank, hence bank poles. Generally, we would set out 25 to 30 poles just before dark with bait and would check them a couple of hours later.

Mom would have supper ready for us before we went back to the creek.

We would start at one end of the bank poles and check them to the other end. Then we would lie on the bank for an hour or so and check the poles the other way back to our vehicle. The catfish that we caught, we would place in a burlap sack and leave in the creek with the cool water running through the burlap sack.

The next morning we would go, remove the bank poles, come home and clean the fish, and if we had a lot of minnows left over, we would put them on top of the tin shed that was used to house chickens and a cow.

The best minnows for stink bait were big shiners that we seined on the Woods Place on Sandy Creek. I made many pints of stink bait with sweet anise oil in it. If the bait was too dry, I would add mineral oil and if it was too wet, I would add flour.

Melton and I were fishing Sandy Creek and we had just finished setting out some bank poles. When we were walking back to the car, we noticed a skunk. I do not know what possessed us to run up and try to hit the skunk with a minnow bucket, but we did and really paid the price. The skunk raised its tail and sprayed us in the face and on our clothes. While Melton was driving us back to town, I held my head out the window trying to get the sting out of my eyes. When we got home, Mom would not let us in the house. She made us strip and hang our clothes on the clothesline, then gave us some soap and told us to wash outside really well before coming into the house.

I do not know the best solution to get skunk smell off humans, but tomato juice is good to use if you have an animal sprayed by a skunk. Soak the animal with the tomato juice, rub it in and then dry it off. My veterinarian said to use the following mix to remove skunk scent from animals: one-quart hydrogen peroxide, ¼ -cup baking soda and one tablespoon of dish soap.

When I fished with a cane pole on Sandy Creek and there was a snake laying on a brush pile or log, I would take my cane pole with a treble hook on the line and hook the snake. I killed a few snakes this way, but most of them would straighten out the hook.

When I was fishing with Dad and I hooked a big catfish, I remember Dad telling me to play the fish on the cane pole. You were more likely to land the fish if you tire it out before trying to land it.

The biggest catfish Dad said he saw in Sandy Creek was the time we had bank poles set out and Uncle Doyle went with us to check the poles. Dad told me Uncle Doyle lost the fish but he thought it was the biggest catfish he had seen in Sandy Creek. We were on CB Harkins land.

The first time I realized that Dad knew I smoked was when we were fishing with bank poles on Sandy Creek. Eugene and I had set the bank poles out and when we went back to check them, Dad and Uncle Doyle went with us. Dad noticed there were a pack of Winston and a pack of Salem in the front seat with Eugene and me. Dad said "Does Eugene smoke two kinds of cigarettes?" The cat was out of the bag! Dad knew I smoked. Dad did not want my brothers and me to smoke, especially if we played sports.

9
My Love of Hunting

The one person who I fished and hunted with the most in Eldorado was Eugene. We hunted many ponds and Sandy Creek for ducks and hunted many places for quail.

Eugene, his brothers Earl and Andy and their dad A.G. are all deceased, but Mozella, the mother of Eugene is living in a nursing home in Altus, OK and what a pleasure it is to visit with her. She has a phenomenal memory and can remember names much better than anyone I know. She is 92 years old and a very special woman.

Eugene and I hunted Hack Barnard's river land west of town. It had plenty of bobwhite and blue quail. We walked miles chasing those blues. It seemed we would see them running over the next hump or hill, and when we got there, they were running over the next hill. Bobwhite do not run as much as the blue quail, but I think the blues taught the bobs how to run.

Eugene was kin to Lehman Jumper, a farmer east of Eldorado, and we would stop by his place and Lehman would tell us where he had seen quail, so Eugene and I would take off in that direction.

I remember us hunting on Early Freeman land east of Eldorado and Early would say, "While I was plowing over there I saw a covey of quail and you can hunt them, but I have a trap out just south of our house that trap quail for my wife and I to eat, so don't bother that covey."

Glen Braker, Trish's first cousin, was a farmer. He let me hunt quail on his land. If I ran into Glen and he had seen quail on his land, he would tell me where he saw the quail.

I remember drinking coffee with Edwin and Mike Thompson at the Eldorado Café and Edwin would tell me he saw a covey of quail on one of his properties while he was sowing wheat and I could hunt that covey.

Terry White has a farm northwest of Eldorado and I would stop and visit with him if I was in his area. Terry walked many, many miles with his boxer named Max on those sandy roads and he would tell me areas he had seen quail.

Most land around Eldorado is leased for hunting and I do not get to hunt most of those farms, but that is not a bad thing because it provides revenue for them and also, land they know they have a place to hunt with family and friends. There are a handful of farmers that I took crappie I caught on Grand Lake that let me hunt their land. I appreciate families like Terry White, Joe Collvin, Don Weaver, Edwin Thompson, Glen Braker, Elmer Shirley, and George "Preacher" Miller. I remember Don made some delicious chocolate-covered coconut candy each Christmas and gave to Trish and me. What a treat!

I took Kris, Heath and one of their friends, John Human, hunting turkey in Eldorado. We were east of Eldorado and we started chasing some turkeys, but Heath and John stayed back and let Kris and I chase them. Well those turkeys flew back toward Heath and John and actually ran close enough to them to get a shot, but both boys were asleep on a sunny hump and did not even know the birds had run by them. Kris had killed one turkey and when I went to the gyp mill intersection to leave the remains for varmints, I spotted some turkeys on the gyp mill property. I went back, got Kris, and told him to drive to the road north of the gyp mill. I walked across the gyp mill land and chased the turkeys down the fencerow where Kris was hiding. Kris shot one when they got to him and I got one when a big gobbler flew back over me.

While in Eldorado, I always enjoyed drinking coffee with great patriots like Richard Griffin. It was a pleasure for me to pay for his breakfast when I checked out. When I worked in Frank Toma Grocery store, Richard would come in and visit. Richard is a big man, very strong and huge hands. I weighed around 150 pounds and Richard would grab me by the head and lift me up; he was that strong.

Earl Dean Taylor and I were fishing on Sandy Creek on the JT Leese land when we saw a squirrel run up a tree and into a hole in a big limb. I decided I could catch that squirrel, even though I did not know what I would do with it after I caught it. I climbed that tree and crawled out on the limb where I could see the squirrel's tail in the hole. I reached in and pulled the squirrel out and it turned and bit me on the hand. I was shaking the squirrel and both of us fell out of the tree, which was about 10 feet high. I did not break any bones, but I did have a bleeding hand. Luckily, I did not get something like rabies. The squirrel ran off and found another tree to climb.

I went squirrel hunting with Dad in Tishomingo, OK once when we visited Clyde Taylor and family. Dad let me use a double barrel 20 gauge shotgun and I remember getting a couple of squirrel for us to clean and eat.

Woodrow and Woody Gibbons, my cousins from Gould, came to Eldorado to hunt some raccoons on the river with their dogs. The only thing I recall finding was a rattlesnake.

I remember there were two people who would furnish me shells if I would kill ducks for them to eat; they were my Uncle Ott and our neighbor Si Williams. Sometimes when I was duck hunting, I would knock down a duck on an ice-covered pond. If the ice were thin, I would take off my clothes, break the thin ice, wade out and get the duck. If there was no ice on the water and the duck was in the middle of the pond, I would throw rocks and wood past the duck to create a wave so it would wash the duck close to the bank. When it got close to the bank, I would pull the duck to the bank with a long branch.

My brother-in-law, Gary, and I were hunting ducks on Uncle Bill and Aunt Ida's land north of Eldorado. Behind a big barn just west of their rented house was a low area that flooded when it rained a lot. There was a fence running through the middle of the area of water and some tumbleweeds caught on the fence. Gary was in the fencerow under a big tumbleweed and I was standing at the corner of the barn. Gary hollered and said he was already out of shells. We had plenty of ducks so we headed to the car that was parked by the house. I got into the car, my dad's 1959 green Chevrolet; Gary followed and sat his shotgun down between us. After he did that, his gun went off and blew a hole through the roof. It scared the daylights out of us! The woman staying there came out, looked at the hole in the roof and said "Ducks aren't worth it, are they?" We did not say anything. I just drove home and listened as Dad told me that I was too big to spank, but not too big to be grounded.

Dad loved to go coyote hunting with local folks and listen to their dogs. They could tell which dog was howling. I went with Dad on several of these hunts.

In high school, some of us would take our vehicles and hunt jackrabbits at night with shotguns on wheat fields. We would take some of the rabbits we killed to a hog farm and give to the hogs. They loved them. It is a wonder that some of us did not get hurt because we ran into ditches and got tossed off the vehicle. The Lord knows the farmers did not want us in their wheat fields driving our vehicles on the young wheat.

Melton and I were hunting quail northwest of Eldorado and were on a sandy road northwest of Hack Bernard's place, when we had a flat. I let my bird dog out while Melton and I fixed the flat. The dog ran behind us on the road and went on point by the side of the road. Melton and I finished fixing the flat and the bird dog was still on point, so we walked back to the dog. There was a group of plum bushes on the side of the road and as I stepped into the bushes, one bobwhite quail flew up and we shot the bird. The amazing thing was that dog was on point for several minutes.

Ricky Hulett, Jimmy, and I hunted quail many days on the Hulett ranch and we killed our fair share. I do not remember how many flats we fixed on Ricky's pickup but it must have been a record because it seemed every time we hunted

their ranch he would run over many cactus or mesquite tree limbs with thorns in them. We ran into holes, trees and anything else that was in our way of chasing those quail. Their place had many coveys of blue quail and those birds loved to run. The best way to hunt them was to bust the covey a couple of times to get them to fly into the side of a rock and grass covered hill, then they seemed to hold and not run. Some coveys of blue quail were very large and we estimated there were 40 to 60 birds sometimes in a covey. It may be that more than one covey got together. I counted as many as 20 coveys in one day of hunting on their place. Ricky's dad, Pill, had around 1,200 acres of land to hunt. Ricky's grandmother, Stella, loved to eat quail, but she did not like quail that had been shot, so we put out traps to catch her quail.

Jimmy and I were hunting quail east of town and a covey flew out into some grass on the Howard place. We walked to where the birds landed and birds started popping up one and two at a time. Jimmy shot five quail standing in one spot, not missing a bird. He was one of the best shotgun shooters I have hunted with.

Jimmy and I were invited on a crane hunt by the Wildlife Department. They wanted to film a hunt on the Red River when the cranes were coming to roost. The cameramen set up their equipment hidden in blinds. We took positions in a blind and waited for the birds. The birds finally showed up and there were plenty of them, but there was a problem. They came in after sundown and you cannot shoot them after sundown. Therefore, you could say, "We didn't get to shoot any cranes and the cameramen didn't get to take any shots of us shooting cranes."

Jimmy, Josh, and I were hunting east of town one cold winter and we came over a hill and heard a cow hollering. We noticed there was a calf that had fallen into a frozen pond. We went to the pond to see what we could do. The pond was frozen pretty thick but the 400 pounds calf was half in the water and half on the ice and could not move. I went back to the truck and found an extension cord. I tested the ice to make sure it was strong enough to hold me. Jimmy and Josh held onto one end of the extension cord. I walked out on the ice, lassoed the calf and walked back to the dam. The three of us gave a big jerk and pulled the calf up on the ice and then it was pretty easy to pull the calf to the dam. We left the calf with its mom and went to town to tell the farmer, Junior Gunkel, what had happened. Junior told me the next day that the Mom had licked the calf clean and it was just fine.

One other time I had to use my lasso skills. Dave Patterson and I were hunting quail on the Wesley Hickman place east of Eldorado and his dog fell into a cistern that had trash and water in the well. I found a stiff extension cord in an old barn, tied a loop on one end, lowered it into the well and managed to get it around the dog's head. Dave and I pulled that dog out of the well with several quick pulls on the cord. The dog was a little sore, but wanted to continue hunting.

Leon Williams, my father-in-law, knew the game warden from Gould and often talked with him when we were out hunting quail. The game warden, in jest, would warn Leon that he had better not shoot the quail on the ground because that was illegal. Leon would say, "The rules state you cannot shoot a quail while it is resting on the ground, and when I shoot one on the ground, it is running." Jimmy Crumes, who was a farmer and went quail hunting with us sometimes would say, "I do not shoot quail running on the ground. I wait until they stop and then shoot them."

It was hard to hunt blue quail with a bird dog because the quail ran so much. The bird dog would point, move, point, move and had a problem staying on point. Leon had a bird dog we believe that understood how to hunt the running quail. We saw the dog on more than one occasion, run around the quail and hunt them back to us.

Leon and I were hunting quail on the Mercer land east of town and a covey of blue quail ran into a brush pile. I got on top of that brush pile, would jump up and down and the quail would fly out one or two at a time. Leon and I almost got our limit in that one spot. It was like a shooting trap.

Many times when Heath and I would go quail hunting with Leon, Heath would say, "Grandpa, I see some deer tracks." Leon would respond, "Pick them up and put them in your pocket and we will clean them when we get home." Leon loved to hunt with his bird dogs and he had some good ones throughout his hunting days.

I didn't know we had prairie chickens around Eldorado until one day Leon, Heath and I were hunting quail east of town and a couple of birds flew up and Leon shot one of them and it turned out to be a prairie chicken. Leon put that bird in his freezer with the intention of having it mounted. I think the bird was eventually trashed because I do not remember seeing that bird on the wall.

Grandfather Leon with Heath and friend; First time we saw Junior

Heath and I went quail hunting with Leon and he had some young German Shorthair bird dogs he had brought from Arizona. He asked if I wanted one of the bird dogs and of course, I did. Heath and I were excited about bringing the bird dog back to Tulsa. Trish had not made the trip to Eldorado, so she did not know we were bringing a dog home with us. At first, Trish was against us

having the bird dog, but as time passed, she was okay with it. We thought about many names to call the dog and finally settled on Junior.

Junior turned out to be the best bird dog I ever owned. He loved to hunt birds, both quail and pheasant. If you knocked down a bird, Junior would find it.

He would stay with me until we found the bird. I remember one time that Heath and I hunted Junior for three days straight, so we gave him a day of rest. Heath and I were hunting a Crop Reduction Program (CRP) patch just north of Eldorado and ran into a covey of quail. We knocked down five

Jim taking picture of Junior and Jennie on point

Jodi and Junior on point and hunters ready

Junior on point

quail and could not find one of them. I told Heath to stay there while I went into town and got Junior. I remember him setting in the front seat with me until we got to the CRP patch. Within

Junior on point

Junior on point

fifteen minutes, Junior found all five of those birds. He was that good. I have many memories of him on point and retrieving quail.

Junior got cancer in his right shoulder and my veterinarian said he could remove the cancer by removing his leg and part of his shoulder. That meant he no longer would be able to hunt, or I hunt him until the cancer became too big a problem.

The last time I hunted Junior was on Gary's land northeast of Eldorado. The cancer got so bad the veterinarian recommend that I put him down. The day I put Junior down was one of the saddest days in my life. On my way to work, I took Junior by the veterinarian's office to have him put down. I cried like a baby when I left the veterinarian's office.

Heath and H.T., Junior and Jodi, with mess of quail

The most quail I have shot in the air with one shot is five. It was one Sunday before Trish and I left Eldorado to go back to Oklahoma City, where we lived, when I got a call from Johnny Freeman to see if I wanted to hunt some quail. I told him I could hunt for a couple of hours. It was snowing lightly and there was a dust of snow on the ground. We were driving south of town and noticed a covey of blue quail behind a pond dam. The pond was dry and the quail were getting out of the wind. I walked to the top of the dam and when the quail flushed, they were really close together. I picked out one bird and when I shot, five birds fell out of the air. I had to shoot a couple of them again because it seems that blue quail can run on broken legs. This is my story and I am sticking to it.

Kris and I went deer hunting with Jay and Brett Fiddler at Camp Grubber and we took Jay's motorcycles. It had been a long time since I drove a motorcycle and I laid my cycle over twice on the hunt. Kris was on the bike with me, but he did not get hurt. When I went to work the next Monday, I was very sore.

Some of the best hunting times were when a group of us would go to Eldorado and hunt dove. Heath, Kris, Jeremy, Jerry, Travis and their friends would gather at our old home place and the fun would began, including eating turkey, dove and other good food. We played horseshoes, poker and just enjoyed the camaraderie of the trip.

One spring the Eldorado community was doing a cleaning project of some of the dilapidated properties in town. The boys and their friends volunteered to

Annual Dove Hunt at Konkler place

drive from Tulsa to Eldorado and spend the weekend cleaning up properties. Eldorado furnished tractors, trucks and food. We cleaned several properties and hauled off the debris. It was a win-win situation. I was proud of the boys for their effort and the town looked better.

One fall we were hunting dove on Tommy Hankins place east of Eldorado and there was Kris, Heath, Jeremy, Nic, Bo, JT, Josh, and me. Someone hollered and said, "Count your birds to see if we have our limit." We did and then headed to our vehicles parked on the blacktop road. The game warden was there waiting for us. He asked me

Volunteer cleanup crew: Top Row - Nic, Chris, J.T. Gerald, Gerald's grandson, Travis, Bo; Middle Row - Heath, Jeremy, H.T., Guy, Senior, Ricky, Leon; Bottom Row - Kris, Adam, Mike and Jerry

if I got my limit and I said, "Yes." He asked Nic if he got his limit and Nic said, "I think so." The game warden said, "Let's count them, if you think you have your limit." Thank goodness! Every one of us had just our limit and no fines were issued.

Dalton visited us and wanted to go quail hunting in Eldorado, so he stopped by Carl Richardson's place and got his hunting license. We headed to Larry Coke's place east of town. When we returned to my vehicle there were two game wardens waiting on us. They checked our licenses, and because Dalton had just purchased his license, we did not get into trouble.

I met Guy Marney while working for Amoco and soon found out that we both loved to fish and hunt. Guy's boys, Walt and Mike, were about the same age as Kris and Heath, so we fished and hunted a lot with the boys. We went on many fishing trips to Eufaula to fish for bass. We hunted for quail, with our dogs, around Eldorado. We hunted quail, duck and geese around Sentinel, OK where Guy grew up and his mom still lived. Sometimes we would have Guy, Heath, Walt, Mike and I in the front seat of the pickup and Guy would ask Heath to hold his cup while he poured a cup of coffee. Heath caught onto this trick and held the cup over Guy's lap, in case he spilled the coffee.

I was shot between the eyes from a 12-gauge shotgun by Guy. Actually, I only had one pellet that went through my nose. It happened when we were hunting east of Eldorado with our dogs and boys. The dogs went on point at the edge of a mesquite patch and a wheat field. When the quail flew up, one went between

Guy and me, so he turned and shot the quail behind us and when he did, I felt a tingle on my nose. One of the pellets hit a mesquite tree, ricocheted back and hit me between the eyes. I noticed my nose was dripping blood so I got my handkerchief out and tried to stop the bleeding. I had blood on my hunting vest and my handkerchief was bloody when Guy looked over and saw me. He was surprised to say the least. We got the bleeding stopped and continued hunting. The next day we were hunting and I bent over to pick up a downed quail and my nose began to bleed again. I do not have problems with nosebleeds, so I knew something was wrong.

Steve

Kris and a couple of ducks we shot on Sandy Creek

When I got back to Tulsa I went to an eye, nose and throat specialist and he determined I had a pellet that lodged behind my nose. He operated on me by going up through my nose to extract the pellet. Guy is one of the safest hunters I have ever hunted with, but accidents can happen even when you are careful.

Steve Russell and I went quail hunting in Missouri with Dusty Ensley. His dad, Harold Ensley, was the famous TV personality on *The Sportsman's Friend* show. The Brittany dog we hunted behind was often on his dad's TV show. Steve's dad was a barber for some of the Kansas City Royals baseball players and we went pheasant hunting with one of the players. I got a Christmas card from the baseball player that year with a picture of his bird dog in the card.

Once, Kris and I were hunting duck on Sandy Creek. We were walking to a favorite shallow water crossing when we started to hear ducks just over the bank. We walked over the hump and mallards flew up everywhere.

I did a lot of quail, dove, duck and rabbit hunting around Eldorado. I have walked many, many miles chasing blue quail or trying to find a covey of bobwhite quail. I have hunted many ponds including Sandy Creek, looking for ducks. I killed young jackrabbit and Dad would use the meat to make chili. I killed

many cottontail rabbits especially when there was snow on the ground and Mom would cook them for me. I even hunted rattlesnakes. I did not eat the snakes but I did save the rattles and I have a quart jar full of them.

Darrell Jones, a classmate, and I killed many rattlesnakes around the dens on the Goss and Durham land southwest of town. Ricky Hulett, Chet Bynum, Jimmy, and I hunted the dens on Red River bluffs, south of town from the Troy Freeman land east to the Cotton Carroll land.

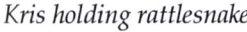

Kris holding rattlesnake

Heath bought a German Shorthair bird dog named Jodi and she had 10 puppies (eight females and two males). One of the males had a marking on him that looked like Mickey Mouse, so I took him and one of the females. We

Chet and H.T. holding rattlesnakes; Dorthell in background

H.T. and Chet holding rattlesnakes

named them Mickey and Minnie. We could not keep Mickey inside our fence, so we gave him to the person from whom Heath bought Jodi. We still have Minnie. She is more of a housedog now than a hunting dog because I do not hunt much anymore. Minnie is a good bird dog and I have several pictures of her on point.

Jerry and I hunted pheasants in Kansas a couple of times but never really did that well. I remember we hunted one field and many of the locals hunted with us. What was unusual was that one of the locals was hunting in a t-shirt and the rest of us were in our insulated suits because there was snow on the ground and it was cold.

Minnie on point

Minnie on point

Another time when we hunted in Kansas, I was with Leon, Heath, and Kris and we were in Leon's pickup pulling his dog trailer. We got on a road that was really muddy and it took all of us to get that vehicle and trailer to a blacktop road. The mud was so bad the tires on the trailer would not roll. It took us a long time at the car wash to get all the mud off the pickup and trailer.

Our first year to hunt pheasant in South Dakota was with Jerry Hurt, Chuck Hurt, Charlie Divens, David Divens, and Les Divens who had family in Aberdeen. That lasted for a couple of years, and then we got down to a core group of Jerry Hurt, Chuck Hendricks, Charlie Hendricks, Matt Smith, Dave Harris, Mike Harris, Kris Konkler, and myself. Others who

Minnie on point

Minnie on point

made the trip on different years were Bob Blake, Travis Hurt, Jeremy Pittman, Nic Debruin, Adam Jobe, George Slunkard, Lester Smith, Troy Cool, Greg Phillips, Jim Shay, Jason Shay, John Shay, Ken Hathcock, and a couple more I did not know.

Most of my pheasant hunting was in South Dakota. We stayed in Aberdeen, SD and generally hunted around Cresbard, SD about 25 miles southwest of Aberdeen. We hunted on places we called the nurse's place, goose lady place, Jones' place, grandpa's place, the elk place and other places we did not name.

Minnie, Mickey and Jodi on point

One of our favorite places was grandpa's place because it had some good shelterbelts, grass and fencerows to hunt. It was next to a place we called the dentist's place, which was owned by a dentist. He kept pen-raised pheasants and released them when he brought in friends and family to hunt. The pen-raised pheasants that left the dentist's place would mix in with the wild pheasants on grandpa's place and we had plenty of pheasants to hunt.

Usually eight of us made the trip each year. We would leave early Saturday morning from Tulsa and get into Aberdeen about 13 hours later. Our limit per day was three pheasants and you could keep five days limit. Generally, we hunted five days and each of us would normally bring home fifteen pheasants.

Qual from day's hunt

South Dakota pheasant hunting near Elk ranch in 2008

You can only shoot the rooster pheasant, as the hen is illegal to shoot. If you accidently shoot a hen, you must leave it in the field. One of our traditions was when a hunter shot a hen pheasant he must wear a 'Hen Shooter' hat to dinner that evening. Chuck followed his dad's footsteps and both of them had to wear the 'Hen Shooter' hat. Charlie tried to hide his hen so we would not know he shot one, but his bird dog retrieved the hen and brought it right to him. I have heard so many reasons for shooting a hen, for example, "The sun was in my eyes and I swear that hen was cackling." (Roosters generally cackle when they fly.) "That hen had the longest tail I have ever seen." (Roosters have long tails and hens do not.)

When hunting pheasants, we stopped hunting around noon and ate a field lunch. Some of the most enjoyable lunches were special sandwiches prepared by my sister, Dorthell. Some brought summer sausage made from deer meat and that was good. We often enjoyed food from Charlie's goodie bag. One year, Jerry brought some smoked salmon. The salmon with cheese and crackers with a cold drink really hit the spot. We also had many lunches at the Fest Inn located in Cresbard, SD.

South Dakota pheasant hunt in 2005: Back Row - Chuck, Charles, Matt.
Front Row - Jerry, H.T. Jeremy, Kris, George

South Dakota pheasant hunt in 2008: Matt, Dave, Troy, Charlie and Chuck

South Dakota pheasant hunt in 2009: Jerry, Cameron, Travis and H.T., with dogs Tish and Sissy

South Dakota pheasant hunt in 2011: Back Row - Greg, Cameron, Dave;
Front Row - George, Chuck, H.T. and Ken

South Dakota pheasant hunt in 2011: Chuck shot a hen today

South Dakota pheasnat hunt in 2008: Charlie shot a hen today

If you accidently shoot a hen, you must leave it in the field. One of our traditions was when a hunter shot a hen pheasant he must wear a 'Hen Shooter' hat to dinner that evening.

10
Studying Pharmacy at Southwestern State College (1962 – 1965)

In the fall of 1962, I started at Southwestern State College, Weatherford, OK, to study pharmacy. In the summer of 1963, I sold Bibles in the Kansas City area for a company in Nashville, TN. In the summer of 1964, I sold Bibles around Marian, IN and in the summer of 1965, I sold Bibles around Lebanon, OH. The family Bible sold for $29.95 and I made a profit of $12.95 off each one of them. I also sold Webster Dictionaries. The dictionaries sold for $9.95 and I made $4.95 off each one of them. One day in Kansas City, I sold 66 dictionaries. The money I made during the summers helped pay my college expenses. I traded some Bibles for guns. I traded for a 22 pistol and a 16-gauge pump shotgun. I traded for a rooster, but had to get rid of it because it kept crowing too early in the morning where we stayed. I traded for a bird dog that was owned by a retired baseball player. His name was Art Herring. He pitched one time against Babe Ruth. Art grew up in Altus, OK and still has relations there. He visited Altus one time and came by Eldorado during quail season looking for me. I was quail hunting and missed visiting with him.

While working in Marian, IN and driving from one town to the next, I was stopped by a local police officer for crossing a yellow line when I passed a tractor on the highway. This local police officer took me to the county seat town, which was Marian, and asked me to pay a fine. I did not have the cash so he let me call someone. I called one of my roommates, who, unfortunately, was not home. The local police officer told me I was only allowed one phone call. I spent that night in jail with 24 other guys who were really bad dudes. Some were in for rape, murder and other serious crimes.

The next morning I told the local sheriff on duty that I needed to call someone, my manager in Nashville, and he was nice enough to let me. Long story short, the Captain of Police felt sorry for me so he bought me breakfast at a nice restaurant and stood up for me when I had to go before a judge to explain the ticket.

September of 1965 I lost my brother, Melton. He was 25 years old. He was electrocuted in Shidler, OK, while working for PSO.

I returned to Southwestern State College to continue my studies. I did not do very well mainly because of the sorrow of losing my brother. I decided it was time for me to join the military service.

11
Fishing While in the Navy (1966 – 1969)

H.T. in Navy from 1966 to 1969

We were in the middle of the Vietnam conflict when I decided to join the Navy. I went to boot camp in San Diego, California, and boarded a ship named USS Jenkins, which was stationed in Pearl Harbor, Hawaii. I journeyed across the Pacific to Yokosuka, Japan. From there I was transferred to a ship named USS Haverfield. I flew from Japan to the Philippines to pick up my new ship. We left from there and went to Vietnam. We patrolled mostly between DaNang and Choli. Our job was to shoot a few rounds of shells into caves whenever needed. We also supported a small fleet of swift boats that was responsible for checking vessels just off the coast of Vietnam. Some of the crew of the swift boats would come aboard our ship to rest and some of us volunteered to take their place while they were on our ship. I did board some trolleys in search for Viet Cong. We captured one Viet Cong and transported him to appropriate authorities.

H.T. in Navy from 1966 to 1969

The Haverfield was involved in a unique situation when we were on duty off the coast of Vietnam. A marine pilot was shot down and killed and he had requested to be buried at sea. Our ship was chosen as the one to perform the ceremonies. I was a Personnelman in the Navy and one of my chores was to handle the administrative work for the Captain and Executive Officer of the ship. The Captain wanted me to take some pictures of the ceremony with his camera. I not only used his camera, but also used mine. I have

Marine pilot shot down and our ship had burial at sea

several pictures of the burial at sea in a scrapbook. We even had a reporter from Newsweek that took pictures and wrote an article in a magazine at the time. I have a copy of that magazine.

On occasion, while patrolling the coast of Vietnam, we would have a 'Holiday Sunday', which meant some of us could relax on the ship. We had fishing poles stored on the ship. I got one of them, trolled behind the ship and caught a 12-pound mahi-mahi. I cleaned the fish and asked one of our cooks to cook the fish for me. It tasted great. When we were moored to the pier in Pearl Harbor in Hawaii, I used the fishing poles to catch bonefish.

Navy "Holiday Sunday" in Vietnam

Another one of our duties while overseas was to be "station ship" in Hong Kong. This meant we have to stay there for several days at a time. We were "station ship" on two occasions. China was just across the bay and several of us involved in sports would go across the bay and play baseball and basketball

Navy playing Chinese students in Hong Kong

against some of the kids in school. One neat thing about the Chinese students in the stands was that they cheered for both teams. It did not make any difference who scored. I have several pictures of my stay in Hong Kong in the scrapbook.

While we were at sea, I got very sick with stomach problems, which turned out to be ulcers. After we got back to Hawaii, the Navy put me in the Army (Trippler) Hospital to determine what to do about my ulcers. They put me on a bland diet and sent me back to the ship, but that did not work, so they sent me back to the hospital. This time, while I was there, I caught hepatitis. I did not turn yellow like the ones who would have jaundice, but my enzyme studies were abnormal.

After a group of doctors examined me for my ulcers, they decided to perform surgery. I was transferred to a Naval Air Station in Corpus Christi, TX to undergo the surgery there, because it was closer to my family. Since I had hepatitis, they waited a while to see if the enzyme counts would go down, but they did not, so surgery was performed.

When stationed at the Naval Air Station, I fished off the end of a pier for croaker, speckle trout, catfish and flounder. Merle Nix and his wife lived in Port just north of Corpus Christi. Merle worked on the base as a civil service worker. His mom lived in Eldorado and somehow he found out that I was stationed there. He would pick me up on the weekend and I would stay with them. He loved to fish the bay by Port for speckled trout and red fish. We used a chrome spoon to catch most of the trout. The chrome spoon had a piece of pink plastic on the ring and it would be knocked off on the first trout we caught, so we tied a piece of pink crochet to the ring. It worked great! Some of the trout would be six pounds, but most of them were around two to four pounds range. We would clean the trout and I would take as much as 30 pounds home with me to Eldorado when I was on leave from the Navy.

While still at the Naval Air Station, the surgeon who operated on me took me to his home, where I saw some of the memorabilia he saved from a tour of duty in Vietnam as a doctor. He had swords, pistols and other things he brought home from Vietnam. When he found out that I was catching trout, he asked me if I would take him and his boys to go trout fishing. The doctor and his boys really enjoyed wading the bay and catching trout.

12
The Love of My Life

Trish and I married on January 16, 1970 in her mother's house in Eldorado, OK. Best man was Ricky Hulett and maid of honor was Betty Taylor.

Trish Konkler

We rented an apartment in Oklahoma City. Trish had just graduated from Oklahoma State University (OSU) with a degree in Office Management and was working as a secretary for Tenneco Oil Company.

You will see Trish's name a lot in this book because she is the 'Love of My Life' and without her love and support, I would not be where I am today. She has sacrificed so much of her life taking care of the boys, me, and her mother.

Trish worked for the Tulsa Public Schools, but decided to quit. She wanted more time to assist her mother, Eula Williams, who has dementia. Trish worked as a secretary at Foster Middle School (now named East Central Junior High), where both of our boys went to school. Even though she decided to quit her full-time work, she still works part-time at the school. Instead of putting Eula in a nursing home or assisted living, Trish and her sister, Shirley, decided to take turns staying with their mother. Trish drives from Tulsa to Eldorado,

Trish Konkler

a 4.5 hours drive and spends two weeks with her mother. She drives back to Tulsa and works for two weeks at the school. Basically, she spends one-half of the year in Eldorado and one-half in Tulsa.

Trish Konkler

Trish understands how much I enjoy the outdoors, especially fishing and hunting. She does not complain about my fishing and hunting trips, what I purchase for fishing and hunting, or all the fin and fowl I keep in the freezer.

When the boys were young, she took the time to go with us on fishing trips even though she does not enjoy fishing. When the boys got older, Trish stopped going. She enjoyed her time to herself. Either she went shopping, saw a movie with her best friend, Judy Stroud, or cleaned the house. Trish took pride in cleaning our house because she always wanted our home to look clean and neat.

Trish had both of her hips replaced and that did not stop her from helping mow our lawn. A joke I told my fishing buddies, "One of my chores is to ensure I keep the blades sharp on our lawn mower so Trish can mow the lawn." I did mow the lawn most of the time though but Trish did more than her share. Eventually, because of Trish's problem with her hips and my problem with leg cramps, we decided to hire someone to mow our lawn.

Trish Konkler

You would think because I love math and have a background of computer science that I would be the one to help the boys with their homework, especially algebra. Nope, it was Trish. She spent many hours reviewing their homework and answering questions the boys would have.

You have heard the expression, 'Two Peas in a Pod'. Trish and her mother are 'Two Peas in a Pod'. They did so many things the same you would think

they were twins, especially before Eula got dementia.

Remember the TV show 'Laugh-In', where in one of the sketches was actress Judy Carne saying, "Sock it to me." When Eula owned and operated the Panther Drive-Inn in Eldorado, we bought her a yellow sweater that was like a dress and the words on it were 'Sock It To Me'. Eula wore that sweater to work.

Trish Konkler

Trish loves her mother just like Eula's other children. I heard her say, "My sole purpose in life is to take care of my mother," and she does. That is one reason she travels 14,000 miles a year going back and forth from Tulsa to Eldorado to stay and take care of her mother.

13
Studying Computer Science at OSU (1970 – 1972)

In January of 1970, I started college at OSU Technical Institute and changed my major from pharmacy to computer programming. I used the GI bill to help pay for college. I worked at a grocery store stocking shelves at night and worked also for a pipefitting outfit on weekends.

One of the guys at the pipefitting place asked me to go duck hunting with him on a farm around Oklahoma City. When we got to the farmer's place, the farmer was drunk and wanted to go hunt the ponds with us. The first fence we came to, I asked for his shotgun. While he crossed the fence, I promptly unloaded his gun without him knowing it. He never knew the difference.

Even though most of my classes were computer related, I had a speech class and I made an A in the class. The professor told me I got the A because I improved the most. To this day, I still have problems with impromptu speeches, but if I can outline and prepare for a speech, I am okay.

After I started to work for Amoco, I gave many seminars to chemical and production engineers, geologists, geophysicists and others. Some had doctorate degrees, but I felt comfortable around them because I knew my topic and I worked hard to ensure I presented the material fully well, so that the software could be used appropriately.

I graduated in computer programming from OSU Technical Institute in the summer of 1971.

I started to go to OSU in Stillwater, OK in the fall of 1971. I took some classes at night. Those days seemed very long. I commuted from Oklahoma City to Stillwater five days a week. Trish had a yellow Volkswagen and it got great gas mileage; that is what I drove to OSU. It was great for driving on roads that had ice, snow or water on them because the motor was over the back wheels and that was great for traction.

Trish and I went to Eldorado to visit around Christmas time. During some Christmas holidays, I worked for Carol Clonts shredding

H.T. graduating from OSU in 1972

cotton stalks. It would be cold, but the little Ferguson Ford Tractor had a cab that was warm inside, and the cotton stalks would not hit me from the shredder.

I took 19 hours one semester and 17 hours in another and in June of 1972, I graduated from OSU with a BS degree in technical education with an emphasis in computer programming.

About a week later, Walt Sellers from Amoco Production Company interviewed me and sent me a job offer. I started to work for them on June 12, 1972 as a computer programmer for $800 a month. Trish and I moved to Tulsa and lived in an apartment until November of 1973, when we moved into the house where we still live today.

14
My Two Sons Kris and Heath (1974 and 1976)

Kris was born on March 27, 1974. Kris graduated from Northeastern State University in Tahlequah, OK, with a degree in Criminal Justice. Kris works for Impact Salvage Solutions in Sapulpa removing dents from vehicle parts.

Heath was born on January 15, 1976. Heath graduated from OSU with a degree in Computer Science. He is working in Bentonville, AR at the main office of Walmart as a Technical Expert. In May of 2003, Heath married Amber Stallings.

While Kris and Heath were in elementary and junior high school, I coached their teams of soccer, baseball, basketball and football. I was the head coach in basketball and assistant coach in all other sports.

Foster Trojans 7th Grade: Back Row - H.T., Mike, Jim, Corey, Heath, Cletus; Front Row - Dustin, Curtis, John, Jason and Martez

Foster Trojans: Row 5 - H.T., Tommy, Cletus, Jerry, Lucky; Row 4 - Corey, Donnie, Trey, Stan, Joe, Travis, Blackburn, Jimmy; Row 3 - Brian, Chris, Curtis, Chad, Jeff, Heath, Dorivan; Row 2 - Dustin, Ryan, Jason, Jimmy, Paul, Matt, Werling; Row 1 - Jeremy, Adam, Travis, Kenny, John, Jason and Wade

15
Amoco Travels

We developed a computer system at Amoco called Technical Computing. I began to give seminars to those who were using the software. I went to Amoco locations in Trinidad, Europe, and in the USA where I gave seminars at the following locations: Tyler, TX; Liberal, KS; Traverse City, MI; Casper, Riverton and Powell, WY and Naperville, IL.

In 1980, I went to Trinidad and gave seminars to engineers on the islands of Trinidad and Tobago. I took the software with me and installed it on their computers. The interface to the software was built with a programming language called PL/1, but the computer operating room in Trinidad did not have that software, so I had to go to an IBM office, get the PL/1 software and install it on their computer. While I was there, I bought the boys some steel panorama drums, which I think was thoughtful at the time. Later on, Trish and I found out that the sound of the boys beating on the steel drums was not a good thing. We eventually stored those drums in the attic until the boys got older and then we gave them to Heath.

In 1981, I went to Europe to install the same Technical Computing software on their computer system and gave seminars to engineers, geologists and geophysicists in London and Great Yarmouth in England, Stavanger in Norway, Amsterdam in the Netherlands and Aberdeen in Scotland.

In Amsterdam, I went to some great museums, a diamond factory, Ann Frank's home, and took a ride on a boat in some of the 200 miles of canals in Amsterdam. We were told that 45 cars a year are pulled from the canals.

In Stavanger, we ate at restaurants that had reindeer on the menu instead of beef. It was very cold in Stavanger and the hotels had feather mattresses that almost smothered you when you got into bed.

In Great Yarmouth, I stayed at a hotel and found out it was my room, which was located at the second floor, that occupants could go through if there was a fire. Outside my door was a glass case with my room key *H.T. in Calgary at Banff Park* inside. In case of fire, they could break the glass case, open my door and go through my closet, which had a door that led outside. Needless to say, I slept with one eye open.

My travels with Amoco were mostly in cities such as Houston, Calgary, and Chicago. I have been to several other cities giving seminars on technical programs or just for meetings.

In January 1998, Amoco merged with British Petroleum and our company was named BP Amoco.

In November 1999, BP Amoco decided to outsource their Accounting and Information Technology department; I worked in the IT department. So one Friday in November 1999, I retired from BP Amoco. The next Monday, I started to work for PricewaterhouseCoopers (PwC) doing the same job at the same desk. The main difference is that I got a year severance check, took a lump sum retirement versus a monthly annuity and continued doing the same work at the same pay.

IBM bought out the part of PwC that I worked for, so from October 1, 2002, I started to work for IBM doing the same job at the same desk. My job title was Project Manager/Coach. I mostly managed a project to get it approved and then managed the project with those who actually did the work to get the project completed. Some projects had over 100 analysts working on the project. I also supervised five employees and was responsible for their work and salary administration.

16
Amoco Bass Club

The first bass tournament I fished was an Amoco Bass Club tournament on Eufaula in 1973 and I was fishing with Don Marple. The first night tournament I fished was an Amoco Bass Club tournament on Tenkiller and I was fishing with Bill Brown.

I fished 143 tournaments in the Amoco Bass Club. I won 51 of those tournaments, came in second, 26 times, third, 19 times and fourth, seven times. Each tournament we drew for partners. I fished with 42 different partners.

Amoco Bass Club fished Truman Lake in Missouri several times. One time Ron Norick and I were partners and we did well. What I remember most is that we had three flats while we were at that tournament.

Jim Manning and I were partners once at Truman, and Amoco Bass Club was fishing there after a big BASS Tournament. I knew Tommy Biffle. Each day they weighed-in, I would go by and talk with Tommy. He told me to check with him after the tournament and he would tell me where he was catching his bass. He told me he caught some of his fish in Little Tebo in the middle of cedar trees. I tried doing that and caught an eight-pound bass right in the middle of a cedar tree. I do not know how I managed to get that bass out without it getting tangled, but Jim dipped that bass in a net just as she came out.

Amoco Bass Club had a deal that if someone caught a bass that was eight pounds or bigger that the bass club would pay for half the mounting cost. I took the bass to Bassel Kirk north of Tulsa and had him mount the bass. This mount is on the wall of our lakehouse on Grand.

I remember fishing with Doug Brown on Truman. He loved to throw a Long A jerkbait and he caught a lot of bass on that

H.T. with 8-lb bass in Amoco Tournament in Truman Lake

bait. I did well with that bait also but today I do not use it anymore and I do not know why. I have many types of bait that I did well on in the past but somehow they were put away because I am always persuaded to use the newest bait on the market. We fishermen are easy targets for the 'latest and greatest'.

Amoco Bass Club had a tournament on Sardis, and the wind was blowing very strong especially on the ramp. Anglers would wade into the water and help catch the boats when we drove them on our trailers. Some of the boats were filled with water and the tires on the trailers looked flat.

H.T. at work at Amoco with bass mounts he caught

Cliff Stoops and I were fishing an Amoco Bass Club tournament on Sardis when a storm came up. Because there was lightning, we decided to park my boat under the Anderson Creek Bridge. There were other boats under the bridge with us. After a while, it appeared that the storm had blown through, so Cliff and I went back to a flat where we were catching bass. Out of nowhere, a lightning bolt came out of the sky and hit so close to us that the hair on my arms stood up and it felt like something pushed me down. I cranked up that 200 HP Mercury Motor on my Champion Boat and headed right back to the bridge.

I was fishing with Harold Harrison in an Amoco Bass Club tournament on Hudson and I noticed he had tied his rod and reel to my rail on the boat while he was fishing. I asked him why. He said that he had thrown a rod and reel in the lake and he did not want to throw any more in the lake. The same day, Harold got hung and was pulling on the line when the lure came flying back hitting one of his teeth and breaking it.

Paul Thomas and I fished an Amoco Bass Club tournament on the navigation channel. We put in at the Little Greenleaf Ramp and we were fishing cuts up river on right side. I threw a yellow/black spinnerbait; it stuck a bass and came back with a strip of meat. I had hooked the bass inside its mouth, but I did not catch the bass. We fished out of the cut, turned around and started fishing back into the cut. We were catching good bass. I casted back in where I lost the bass and caught the same bass I missed. I know it was the same one because it was bleeding inside its mouth where a strip of skin was missing.

Kris and I fished an Amoco Bass Club tournament on Eufaula. I caught a four-pound smallmouth on a clown-colored jerkbait. We had our limit so I stopped on the point where I caught the four-pounder and hooked the biggest smallmouth I have ever hooked. I believe it was over seven pounds. I was using eight pounds test line and had my drag set properly. One pass by the boat Kris dipped the net and that bass went down. The problem was one of the treble hooks was caught in the net and the bass straightened out the hook that was in its mouth. We were sick, but that is one reason fish get big. We lose them. We came in second in the tournament.

Ken Mason and I fished an Amoco Bass Club tournament on Eufaula and were fishing the chute in a cove we call the pipeline cove. We were fishing secondary points and using jig/chunk. It seemed there was a big fish on every point. We went down the lake to another cove and I was fishing same pattern when we ran into Bob Austin and his dad who were fishing our tournament. Bob told me we should be throwing a jerkbait because they were catching them good on that bait. Bob was a very good friend and we did not mind sharing information even when we were fishing a tournament. When they fished past us, I threw my jig/chunk on the point and caught a four pounder. We won the tournament.

John Carter and I fished an Amoco Bass Club tournament on Eufaula and we were fishing the pipeline cove. I was fishing a wind-blown point when my trolling motor hit a stump and I stepped off the front of the boat in my insulated suit. After I got back into the boat, I kept on fishing in the cold wet clothes. We tournament fishermen will hardly stop fishing a tournament even when it makes common sense to do so.

I fished an Amoco Bass Club tournament on Fort Gibson and was in Choteau Creek when I dropped a rod and reel in the water and could not find it. Heath was in Tulsa and when I came home, he told me he could find it. We went to a ramp near Choteau Creek and put into the water. The water was about six feet deep and within ten minutes of us being there, that boy found the rod and reel. He said he went to the bottom; spread his arms and legs like you would do when making an angel in the snow and he hit the rod with his hand.

While fishing an Amoco Bass Club night tournament on Eucha with Cliff Stoops, I dropped a rod and reel in the lake in 15 to 20 feet of water. Cliff and his wife Debbie scuba dive, so they came back to Eucha and tried to find the rod and reel, but no luck.

In another Amoco Bass Club night tournament on Tenkiller, I managed to kick a rod and reel in the lake. A couple of friends from Amoco who scuba dive, tried to find the one in Tenkiller, but no luck. I did reward the boys for trying by giving them money to take their wives out for a nice dinner.

George Brown and I fished an Amoco Bass Club tournament on Broken Bow, and at the weigh-in, I took the fish to the scales. George was in the boat. When I returned he was sitting against the tire of the trailer. He had fallen out of the boat and had broken his arm. I wanted to take him to the hospital, but he said he would put his arm on a pillow while I drove us back to Tulsa. When we got back to Tulsa, his wife took him to the doctor and sure enough, his arm was fractured and needing to be set and put in a cast. He was about 20 years older than I was and what a tough man!

While at Broken Bow, George and I spent the night in my pickup, which had a camper shell. One night I heard noise. I looked out the camper, and a raccoon was trying to get a lid open on my boat. I scared the raccoon away. Another night I heard noise and I saw two raccoons getting food out of trash containers. The park rangers had spring-loaded trash containers and one of the raccoons would hold the lid open while the other one jumped down into the trash container and took out any food it could find.

The best tournament I have had fishing a crankbait was with Cliff Stoops on Fort Gibson fishing an Amoco Bass Club tournament in 1990. We were using a firetiger-colored 6A Bomber crankbait. We had two bass that weighed six pounds and three more good ones. We won the tournament.

Jeremy and I fished an Amoco Bass Club night tournament on Grand. That morning when we came back to the spillway ramp, the wind was blowing very hard and anglers were having problems loading their boats. As a matter of fact, one angler's boat got close to the cable by the spillway. His motor quit and the wind flipped the boat over the cable and it sank. Luckily, the angler was wearing a life jacket and the gates were not open. He was bobbling up and down like a cork against the dam. I loaded my boat, grabbed a rope from my vehicle, lowered it down to the angler, and then pulled him to shore. That was the last tournament that angler fished.

Amoco Bass Club had a tournament on the navigation channel at Little Green Leaf Ramp and I drew Doug Brown as a partner. My problem was I also was coaching Heath's football team Saturday morning. I let Doug pull my boat to the lake, coached Heath's game, and then I got into my vehicle and drove to the bass tournament. When I got to the ramp, Doug was waiting for me and he already had a limit of five fish. We culled a couple before the end of the tournament and won the tournament.

H.T. was given a plaque from his Foster team because he fished in tournaments a lot

An accountant at Amoco, Bill Smart, called me one Sunday after Trish and I had returned from church and asked me to go fishing on Hudson with him. We launched from Wolf Creek Ramp and fished in the back of the creek. There were metal signs nailed to trees with the word 'Channel' on them, so it was easy to follow the channel. Over the years, I have caught many bass on laydowns, stumps and trees that lined the channel. That day we caught many bass on a spinnerbait. Bill taught me really how to fish with a spinnerbait. He fished with a yellow/black skirt and a three-inch yellow plastic trailer on his spinnerbait in muddy water. He fished a white spinnerbait in clear water. Today I fish a yellow/black spinnerbait in muddy water and a chartreuse/white otherwise. I have other colors, but these are my 'go to' baits.

Bill took me toward the pumpback station bridge, stopped on the left before getting to the bridge and fished some stumps and an old concrete house foundation. Then he went under the bridge and pointed out some seagulls flying on the east bank. That signaled that there was baitfish in the area. We fished some stumps on the east bank, Bill ran toward the pumpback station and we fished a laydown tree in the middle of the cove. In all of these places, we caught good bass on the spinnerbait. As we were heading back to the ramp, he stopped at the riprap by the bridge. He tossed a white crankbait with a little pink on it and caught a nice bass. That was the only time he tossed a crankbait and we did not fish that spot over 10 minutes.

17
Fishing The Annual Children's Tournament

The Amoco Bass Club and other Amoco employees would volunteer to take children fishing to the Annual Children's Tournament on Keystone Lake. These were children from boys' homes, girls' homes and hospitals.

About a week before the tournament, we would take hog pellets and bait different coves to draw carp into the area. We did this several times before the tournament started. On tournament day, each Amoco boat was given some hog pellets to chum the water. Most of us used the wheaties/strawberry pop concoction and caught many pounds of carp. The children loved it because it was easy to catch fish and they caught lots of them.

Amoco sent a reporter from Chicago to write a story about the tournament.

Annual Children's Tournament

Annual Children's Tournament

Amoco empoyess taking children fishing in the A.C.T.

Annual Children's Tournament

18
Names of Bass Clubs and Major Tournaments I Have Fished

(Partner's name is in brackets)

Amoco Bass Club (I fished with 42 different partners)

Charger Tournament on Truman (Kris Konkler)

Fish-N-Force Team Trail (Rick Newman, Dave Patterson)

Grand Challenge on Grand (Heath Konkler)

Great Catch on Grand (Heath Konkler)

McDonald Douglas Bass Club (Jay Fiddler)

Northeastern Bass Anglers Bass Club (Larry Moffett, Pat Murphy)

Okiebass Bass Club (Pat Murphy)

Oklahoma State Championship on Grand (Larry Moffett, Heath Konkler)

Old Timers Bass Club (Tom Stewart)

Poor Boys Bass Club (John Lorenzo)

Skeeter Team Trail (Dave Patterson, Heath Konkler)

Strike King Bass Club (Larry Moffett, Cliff Stoops, Heath Konkler)

The Last Bass on Eufaula (Heath Konkler)

Tulsa Metro Bass Club (Larry Moffett, Heath Konkler)

Tulsa Southside Hookers Bass Club (Rick Newman, Heath Konkler, Kris Konkler)

19
Fishing Bass Tournaments

The first time I fished Sardis was with Jay Fiddler in the McDonald Douglas Bass Club. We fished a two-day classic and after the first day, we were in fifth place. The second day we went to Jack Fork North Creek and the area looked just like Old Mexico Lake Guerrero, so I tied on a ½ ounce white spinnerbait. We began to catch some really big bass. There were a couple of old timers fishing on the other side of trees we were fishing. One of them asked me what I was using for bait. I said it was a white grub. Just before we left for weigh-in, the gentleman told me he was getting hung fishing the grub. I told him to put a white spinnerbait on front of the grub. We won the classic.

Jay and I fished a McDonald Douglas Bass Club tournament on Fort Gibson. When I was backing my boat off the trailer, I put the boat into reverse with the motor running too fast. It broke the shaft on the motor. We put the boat back on the trailer, drove back to Tulsa, got Jay's boat and fished the tournament.

Jay and I fished a McDonald Douglas Bass Club tournament on Tenkiller. We were fishing in the back of a cove below Cherokee Ramp. Water was running in the back of the cove. Right on the mudline (a place for fish to hide and catch bait), I was throwing jig/chunk and I caught a couple of good ones and we won the tournament.

Jay and I fished a McDonald Douglas Bass Club tournament on Keystone. Before we fished the tournament, I talked with a friend, Ray Weaver, because he knows Keystone very well. Ray told me about the bank where the river was close and fish were holding around big boulders. We slow-rolled a yellow/blue spinnerbait around those boulders and caught several bass. Our first pass on that bank we caught five bass over three pounds each. We culled to a big stringer and won the tournament.

Jay and I fished a McDonald Douglas Bass Club night tournament on Grand. We started in the back of Honey Creek fishing a buzzbait on some stumps. The lake was up a little. I caught a five-pounder off those stumps. We moved out to some boat docks and I tossed a jig/chunk over a cable and out came a nice four-pounder. I ran to Long Resort boat dock, went under a cable, tossed my jig/chunk toward some wood pilings and caught a six-pounder. We were on a roll. Later that night, we went back under Honey Creek Bridge and fished behind the lighted docks on the right side of the creek. The bass were there and we caught them on a black spinnerbait and jig/chunk. We won the tournament.

Jay and I fished a McDonald Douglas Bass Club night tournament on Eucha. It was raining and he went to sleep sitting in a boat seat. I continued fishing. I was slow-rolling a black spinnerbait and catching the bass in the weeds. The first cut on the left of Eucha cove was a big tree off the point. Jay caught a six pounder that night on a jig/chunk. The next morning Jay caught a six pounder out of the same tree slow-rolling a spinnerbait. We won the tournament.

Jay and I fished a lot of McDonald Douglas Bass Club tournaments and whenever we had a night tournament or a two-day tournament, we took one of our pickups that had a camper shell. The biggest challenge was who could go to sleep first. We both snored really badly.

The only angler I have ever seen jerk the lips off a bass was Jay. We were fishing a McDonald Douglas Bass Club tournament on Hudson and we were in Clendenon Creek. By the time we fished in and back out of the creek, we had our five fish limit. What was amazing was at the mouth of the creek Jay set the hook on a small spotted bass and actually jerked the lips off the bass. We culled every one of the fish in the livewell when we went to Cabbage Hollow and fished the slough. There was a place where the river cut to the bank and created an eddy. I caught three four-pound bass in a row in the eddy. Jay also caught a four-pound bass in the eddy. We won the tournament.

Jay Fiddler and I did well in the McDonald Bass Club. Later on, I found out from Dennis Huggins that he and Kippy Morrow followed us around to see where we were catching bass.

Larry and I fished many bass tournaments on Eufaula and we would generally stay with his in-laws, the Bakers. Because I snored a lot, Larry would put me in a different room from where he slept. That was before I got my CPAP machine for sleep apnea.

Larry and I fished a Northeastern Bass Anglers Bass Club tournament on Keystone and were fishing up above Walnut Creek, fishing main lake stuff. We were using a seven-inch worm in a camouflage color. We caught enough bass to win the tournament. One thing I remember as we ran down the lake I heard a thump. A big bass had jumped and knocked open the livewell door. The bass was flopping in the splash well area and just before the bass made it back into the lake, Larry jumped on the bass and put it back into the livewell.

Larry and I fished a two-day Northeastern Bass Anglers Bass club classic tournament on Grand. After the first day, we were in fifth place. The last bass we caught that day was in a cut up the Neosho River. We started there the next day and caught a couple of solid bass. We then ran further up the river and began fishing laydowns on bluffs. Our boat was in 25 feet of water and we were fishing chartreuse/white spinnerbaits in three to five feet of water. Baitfish was thick and flipping a lot. We fished each shallow cut. If we did not get a bite, we would make another pass in the cut. We had a five fish limit by 9:00 A.M., so we just kept fishing the shallow cuts and weighed-in 19 pounds that day, which was enough with the first day catch for us to win the classic.

Larry and I were fishing a three-day tournament on Eufaula. Top 30 teams from the first two days made it to the championship's final day. We tied for 30th place, but tie breaker was the team with the most fish. We had nine bass and the other team had 10 bass. The team that beat us went on to win the tournament. The final day everyone started at zero weight. I lost a three-pound bass on a boat dock when I tossed a worm over some Styrofoam under a walkway. That fish would have put us in the final day and no telling how we would have finished in the championship.

Larry and I fished a 109 boat Lions Club bass tournament on Hudson. We launched from Wolf Creek. Larry and I started in the back of Wolf Creek with him throwing a jig/chunk and I throwing a yellow/black spinnerbait. We had a nice limit and made a run to the turn-around riprap by Spavinaw Creek. I tossed the spinnerbait over a laydown and a big bass took off and I stuck the bass, but she came up and spit out the bait. It looked to be five pounds or bigger. We finished second, but what I remember was a local photographer was taking our picture for the local newspaper. Some local, who was not fishing the tournament, came up to us and was saying, "You did not win, you did not win." I do not know why he did that and I did not want to find out.

The biggest bass I have ever caught was in an Okiebass Bass Club tournament with Pat Murphy on Lake Tenkiller. It was on a Sunday and I had to leave for the airport after the tournament to fly to San Francisco for a business meeting. Pat had pre-fished the lake on Saturday and found some good bass in the back of Burnt Cabin Creek. The lake was up eight feet. Water was everywhere including flooded buckbushes. He started with a spinnerbait and I was throwing a jig/chunk. I hooked a big fish in the buckbushes but it got off. About two hours later, we came back to the same area and I hooked a 9.29-pound bass. It got me hung in the buckbushes, but I was lucky and landed the fish. When I stuck this fish, Pat would say, "Give it some line." I did, and that fish was wound all through the buckbushes. The line got tight and I thought I had just lost another big bass. I looked into the bushes and saw a little white spot,

H.T. with 9.29-lb bass caught in Okiebass Bass Club Tournament on Tenkiller in 3/8/97

which happened to be a spot on the bass' lip. I had an insulated suit on, so I rolled up my sleeve, reached into the cold water and found the lip on that bass. I clamped down very hard on its lip and pulled the bass out of the buckbushes. I hurriedly put the bass in the livewell thinking it was eight pounds or so. We lost more big fish that day but weighed-in the big one. We took a picture of the bass, the director of the tournament and me; after that I released the bass back into the lake.

Pat Murphy and I fished a two-day Okiebass Bass Club classic tournament on Eufaula. We were leading the tournament after the first day and we were scheduled to be first out on the second day. We were in the boat with about five minutes to takeoff, but I got a gas pain and had to make a trip to the restroom, so we were the last boat to take off even though we were scheduled to take off first. We made it to our best spot where we had caught some fish on a bank by the Highway 40 riprap. We threw a Bomber 7A crankbait. There was a jug floating in the area we were fishing and I hung it with my crankbait. Finally, I got it off my bait and I was going to toss it back in the water. There was a brick tied to the line and a rusty hook was dangling on the jugline. I tossed the brick hard to get it out of our way, but the problem was that the hook buried into the top of my hand. It jerked so hard that the hook made a big cut, so it was easy to remove the hook. I was bleeding very badly. I dipped my hand into the dirty water to get blood off my hand. I had poison ivy on my forearm and it was wrapped in gauze. I used that gauze to wrap around the cut on my hand. By that time, a knot rose about an inch high on my hand. Pat asked if I wanted to go to the emergency room and I said "No." We ended in second place and were beaten by our friends, Larry Moffett and Ray Weaver.

Pat and I fished an Okiebass Bass Club classic tournament on Eufaula and we had located some bass in the back of Fame Creek. The lake was up so we could fish a long way into the creek. We were catching bass when another boat came toward us. Just before they got to us, I tossed my worm by a brush pile and I got that magical thump. I told Pat and he told me not to set the hook because we did not want them to know we were catching fish. We missed getting a check by a small amount and I think the bass I had hit might have given us enough weight to get a check.

Cliff Stoops and I were fishing a Strike King Bass Club tournament on Hudson. We were in my Champion Boat and 200 HP Mercury. When I began to leave Wolf Creek, a piston went through the motor. We were dead-in-the-water. I used the trolling motor to get to a ramp, and then have someone come get us. I sold that boat, just as it was, to Bob Slepka, an Amoco friend. Bob got the motor fixed and kept the boat at his place on Grand. When I fished Grand, I would see Bob running around the lake in my old boat.

The last night bass tournament I fished was a Southside Hookers Bass Club tournament with Don Buchanan on Tenkiller. I lost my wallet that night when I got out on the bank to use the restroom. A man from Oklahoma City found it later and gave me a call. He mailed my wallet to me with everything in it, even the money was still inside it. I sent him $100 and told him to take his family out for a great dinner.

Rick and I have won our fair share of tournaments on Fort Gibson, whether it was up river, main lake points, in the bays, or in a creek. Tommy Biffle is a BASS pro and lives on Fort Gibson. Rick and Tommy fished Fort Gibson many times when they worked at Ford Glass Plant. I got the benefit of fishing some of Tommy's fishing holes on Fort Gibson.

Rick and I fished a Tulsa Southside Hookers Bass Club tournament on Grand. I had pre-fished the lake and found some bass around Red 11 area. The lake was up and we started under the bridge at Red 11. Rick caught a five-pound bass, then we ran to Wolf Creek and Rick caught a 3.5-pound bass. We then ran to Horse Creek and really got on them. I was throwing a chartreuse/white spinnerbait and Rick was throwing plastic. I caught a six-pounder beside a log. Then I tossed my spinnerbait by a good looking laydown tree on the bank. I got hung in the tree and I was making noise trying to get the bait loose. Rick told me to wait and let him throw his bait by the tree. He caught a four pounder even after I made all that commotion of shaking the tree. We won the tournament. When we weighed-in there was a team ahead of us and they had 21+ pounds. The tournament director was taking their picture when I stepped to the scales. We had 22+ pounds. The other team said something like, "Aw, shoot!"

Rick and I fished a Tulsa Southside Hookers Bass Club tournament on Eufaula. I was throwing a jerkbait on a riprap when I hooked something. I thought I was hung, until the fish started swimming to deep water. I fought the fish for a while before we got a look at it. It was a drum that weighed 20+ pounds. That was the biggest fish I have caught on a jerkbait.

Rick and I fished a Tulsa Southside Hookers Bass Club tournament on Hudson. I went to Wolf Creek and ran the roadbed through the timber. I had run this path many times, but this time I turned on the flat too early and hit a big stump with a lower unit of the 200 HP Mercury Motor. That ended our tournament. I had to get someone in the creek to take me to the Lions Club Ramp. I drove my truck and trailer to a ramp in Wolf Creek and loaded my boat.

Rick and I fished a Tulsa Southside Hookers Bass Club classic tournament on Hudson. We were leading the tournament after the first day and had a heavy stringer the second day. My cranking battery would not start the motor because the cables were melted to the battery. We tried to get the cables off the cranking battery so we could use the trolling motor battery to start the motor, but we could not. Luckily, there was another boat in the cove we were fishing. They took our catch and me to the weigh-in. We won the classic. I pulled my trailer to the back of the cove and we loaded the boat from an old ramp.

When Rick and I fished a Fish-N-Force Team Trail Tournament, one of our sponsors was Tommy Thompson and he donated $1,000 to each tournament for prize money. Rick and I fished in a Fish-N-Force Team Trail tournament on Hudson and we won the tournament and thought we had caught a big bass for the tournament. Another team caught and weighed-in a bigger bass, but they had not put in their entry fee for the big bass. Tommy decided to give two big bass cash prizes because he did not want either team to be disappointed. I wrote Tommy a letter thanking him for being a sponsor of the Fish-N-Force Team Trail.

Rick and I fished a Fish-N-Force Team Trail tournament on Grand and put in at Martin's Landing. We ran to Horse Creek and Rick began to fish the riprap with a Bandit Series 200 crankbait. The wind was blowing hard and Rick caught a nice keeper on the first cast so I took his fish off while he stayed on the trolling motor. Rick caught five keepers before I made a cast. I would take the fish off his bait, weigh it, put a float on its lip and put in the livewell. I did manage to catch a couple of bigger bass that we used to cull some of the first bass that Rick caught. We won the tournament.

The very next tournament Rick and I fished was the Fish-N-Force Team Trail tournament on Eufaula. We were fishing Brooken Cove and our pattern was to throw a small spinnerbait in the weeds. Normally I don't like to throw a small spinnerbait less than 3/8 ounce, but that day I used a 1/4 ounce because the baitfish were about that size. That was the smallest spinnerbait I have fished a tournament. We won the tournament.

I fished a Fish-N-Force Team Trail tournament with Rick on Grand. We won the tournament but I did not get a bite all day. We were fishing in my boat and I was in front. Normally the front partner has best chance to catch a fish because they have the first shot at a target. He was throwing a spinnerbait and sweet beaver plastic bait. He put it on me good, but I really was not disappointed. I just wish I could have been more of a help.

Rick and I fished a Fish-N-Force Team Trail tournament on Grand and I threw a rod and reel in the lake in 20 feet of water. I did not find that one either. I had one of my favorite suspended jerkbaits tied on and so that was a special loss. Smithwick does not make that trout color anymore.

Rick and I fished the Fish-N-Force Team Trail tournament on Tenkiller after the tornado hit Oklahoma City in May 1999. I was very tired because Trish and I were up most of the night hiding in our closet because the tornado was heading toward Tulsa. On our way home from the tournament, I fell asleep while driving and I ran off the Muskogee Turnpike just west of Hwy 69. I bounced off the exit on ramp and headed toward center concrete barriers. Somehow, I turned the truck and with boat attached, slid off into the grassy ditch and headed in the opposite direction I was going. It peeled the tires off my trailer and broke the nylon tie-downs on the trailer, but the boat stayed on the trailer. My truck had $6,000 damage. My boat and trailer were totaled. Good news was neither Rick nor I were hurt. Rick was sleeping, but he woke up when his head hit the passenger side window.

My-brother-in-law, Jerry, and I went to Fort Gibson and put out some brush piles in a bay. Later, Rick and I fished a Fish-N-Force Team Trail tournament and we caught some good bass from those brush piles. I lost a big one over those brush piles on a spinnerbait because my drag was too loose when I set the hook. That cost us the tournament. We finished second.

Rick and I were Anglers-Of-The-Year in 2004 and 2005 in the Fish-N-Force Team Trail. We were leading in points in 2006 but the last tournament we did not weigh-in a fish. We caught about 15 bass that day, but none of them were 14 inches long. One fish would have given us 10 more points for the year. We finished second for AOY with 482 points. The winners had 484 points. The ironic thing is we should have won the tournament because we had one bass in the livewell that I think was just barely 14 inches long. When I went to get a weigh-in bag, I noticed an official, I thought was a game warden. 'If you keep (weigh-in) a bass under the legal limit, you can get fined,' and that was on my mind when I went back to the boat to measure the bass again. Rick told me it was my call as to whether to weigh the fish or toss it back. Without thinking too much, I tossed the bass. To this day, I still think that bass was 14 inches long.

H.T. and Rick Newman
Angler of Year in 2004 and 2005 in
Fish-N-Force Team Trail

David McCoy was the tournament director and was sure we had won AOY for 2006. David told me he was going to get us something different from jackets. Each AOY winner gets a jacket with his name, date, Fish-N-Force Team Trail and Angler of Year on it. We also get free entry fees the following year, so quite a bit of money was involved. I have always wondered what David would have given us instead of the jackets.

Heath and H.T. won Strike King Bass Club Tournament on Sardis

One cold spring day, Heath and I fished a Strike King Bass Club Tournament on Sardis. We won the tournament with only two bass. There were only four bass weighed-in. Heath caught both bass on a black/yellow spinnerbait in very muddy water. One weighed 6.45 pounds and the other weighed 4.60 pounds.

Each November Heath and I fish The Lass Bass tournament on Eufaula. One year we finished second and won $7,000. Heath caught one of the hourly big bass at 6.64 pounds and we received an additional $625 for that. A couple of other years we won $1,000. This past year we missed getting a check by .67 pound.

Heath and I fished a big bass tournament called Bob Sealy's American Fishing on Grand. Heath caught the second largest fish of the tournament; he won $400 for catching the hourly big bass. Because we were able to weigh the bass in at noon, and Heath was wearing a special t-shirt, he won another $400.

Heath caught 6.64-lb bass in The Lass Bass Tournament and won hourly prize

Heath lives in Bentonville, AR and on New Year's Day, he asked me to fish a

Heath catches 6.12-lb bass in Bob Sealy's American Fishing Tournament for Big Bass in May 1995

tournament on Beaver with him. I have done that a couple of times. The weather is pretty cold that time of year. It was hard to believe that 60 teams will get out in that kind of weather to go fishing. Also for some reason we always have trouble beating Steve Meador in that tournament. That boy can catch them.

Heath and I fished a Tulsa Southside Hookers Bass Club night tournament on Tenkiller. On his way to the lake from Arkansas, he stopped and got a sandwich to eat. He got food poisoning from that sandwich and threw up most of the night. He just lay on the back of the boat and groaned. I even had to land a big fish without his help because he was so sick. Luckily, by morning, he was feeling better and we found some big fish on buzzbait and won the tournament.

H.T. and Heath won The Great Catch Tournament on Grand in April 2008 with 26.1 lbs

On April 5, 2008, Heath and I fished The Great Catch on Grand. The tournament was on a Saturday. I pre-fished on Wednesday by myself. I fished four hours and did not get a bite. The lake was high and I fished the flooded willows with a spinnerbait. Heath came to the lake on Friday. We started fishing down lake and caught a couple of three pounders on spinnerbait. We started fishing the main lake and Heath caught a six-pound, nine-ounce bass on a RC 2.5 crankbait. We took a picture and released her back into the water. Five minutes later I caught a six-pound five-ounce bass slow rolling a spinnerbait. We got off that bank and began looking for a second pattern. We caught some more fish but nothing like the two big ones. The tournament allowed us to launch anywhere, but we could not start fishing until start time. We were on the good bank and started fishing at 8:00 A.M. On

Bass fishing: The Great Catch Open drew 245 boats to Grand Lake last weekend, where teams found pretty good spring fishing. There were numerous five-bass limits weighed and Heath and H.T. Konkler of Bella Vista, Ark. and Tulsa won $3,650 for 26 pounds, 1 ounce and there were several 7-pounders caught.

This event was staged by the Skeeter Tour officials, but was an extra meet, not part of their regular circuit. Skeeter Tour visits Grand again April 20, and Carolina-rigged lizards are reportedly very effective there now, along with the traditional spinnerbaits and jerk baits.

Write-up about winning with 26.1 lbs

my first cast, I caught a fish but it was a small non-keeper. They say it was a bad omen to catch a bass on the first cast, but I disproved that myth. By 9:00 A.M. Heath and I had our five fish limit. By 11:30 A.M., we had 26.1 pounds on five bass and we won the tournament. Heath had the big one at seven pounds and I had two six-pounders. We caught more keepers but could not cull our smallest bass, which was 3.5 pounds. This was the most pounds of bass I have weighed-in a tournament.

Heath and I fished a Strike King Bass Club tournament on Keystone and the lake was high. We went to Salt Creek and in the very back end of a cove there was a waterfall. Normally you could not get to this spot. We would throw our bait on top of the waterfall and pull it into the pool below the waterfall. The bass were stacked in there and we caught enough big bass to win the tournament. We were fishing a jig/chunk and the pool was about three feet deep.

Heath and I fished a Strike King Bass Club tournament on Keystone and we caught the bass on a Zara Spook Jr. We were fishing riprap. We won the tournament.

Heath and I fished a Southside Hookers Bass Club tournament on the navigation channel. Take off was at the ramp just west of Wagoner on the Verdigris River. Tournament Director allowed us to trailer so I traveled to 3-Forks Ramp and put in there. Heath lives in Bentonville, AR, so he drove to 3-Forks Ramp and we took off from there. When we got ready to weigh-in he drove back to Arkansas. I drove back to the weigh-in ramp, but I ran into a problem. A train was on the railroad crossing at 3-Forks and there was no way to go around the stopped train. It seemed forever before that long train moved. I drove the turnpike over the speed limit. Thankfully, no Highway Patrol was working that area that day. I just barely made the weigh-in on time. We did not win, but we did place high and got a check.

H.T. catches big bass on A-rig pre-fishing for Heath on Eufaula

Heath and I fished The Big Bass Tournament on the Arkansas River in Arkansas. We caught bass, but not the big ones. The one thing I remember was a cottonmouth water moccasin crawled into the big motor. I spent some careful moments getting that snake out of there and not letting it get into the boat.

Heath and Drew Patterson had a Skeeter Team Trail tournament on Eufaula, so

Heath and I pre-fished Eufaula for the tournament. We launched from Duchess Creek and started throwing the A-Rig. The first point we fished Heath caught a seven-pound bass. We continued fishing main lake points and our top five was over 22 pounds. When Heath and Drew fished in the tournament, the weather had changed and the pattern we found was not working. Heath did weigh-in a 6.85-pound bass, but they did not catch their five fish limit.

Heath with 6.85-lb bass caught in Skeeter Torunament on Eufaula

Kris and I fished a 500-team Charger Boat tournament on Truman in Missouri. We were in second place after the first day. We did not weigh-in a fish the second day, but still managed to finish eighth place and win $800.

Kris and I fished a Tulsa Southside Hookers Bass Club night tournament on Fort Gibson. We were awarded a Life Saving Award in 1991 from the Army Corp of Engineer. We were fishing the lights around boat docks in the Rocky Point area of the lake when we heard boats running and kids yelling, then we heard the crash. I told Kris to lift the trolling motor so we could motor out to help. When I got to the first boat, it was a ski boat with two girls in it. One was on the floor and knocked out. The other girl was hysterical. When I asked her how many were in her boat, she answered two, but actually, there had been seven in the boat. The ski boat was hit by a jet boat with five people in it. We knew the ski boat was sinking, so we hooked onto it with the girls still in the boat and pulled it to a ramp by the boat docks. Another boat was hooking onto the jet boat and picking up people who were tossed into the water. While we were at the ramp a 12-year-old boy was checking boats and asking, "Where is my dad, where is Mike?" Kris and I went back out to where the boats collided and found floating tennis shoes and beer bottles, but no Mike. Mike was killed; he was 35 years old. Another male, a 19-year-old man also was killed.

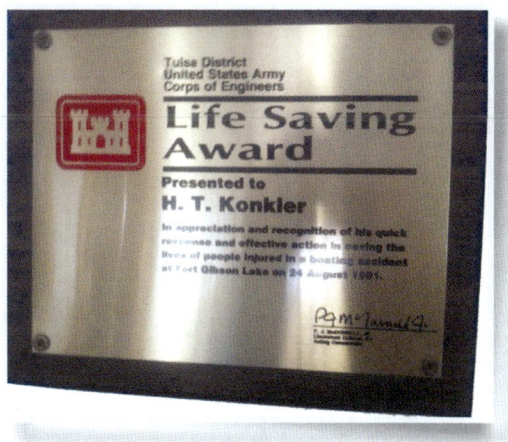

H.T. and Kris receive Corps of Engineer award for rescuing people in boat wreck

After talking with lake patrol and highway patrol, Kris and I did not feel like fishing so we found someone who was fishing our tournament and told them we were going home. I emphasized to Kris, life is precious and it can be gone in a flash. I also pointed out that drinking and driving are very dangerous.

Kris and I had to go to Wagoner County Courthouse and testify what we saw because the person driving the jet boat was charged with manslaughter.

Kris and I also received a letter from the Army Corp of Engineers and a letter from Representative Jim Inhofe.

DEPARTMENT OF THE ARMY
TULSA DISTRICT, CORPS OF ENGINEERS
POST OFFICE BOX 61
TULSA, OKLAHOMA 74121-0061

REPLY TO
ATTENTION OF

Safety and Occupational   December 18
  Health Office

Mr. H. T. Konkler
2012 South 123 East Avenue
Tulsa, OK 74138

Dear Mr. Konkler:

    I am pleased to commend you for rescuing several seriously injured boating accident victims from drowning at Fort Gibson Lake. Your heroic effort and dedicated response was a laudable achievement.

    On August 24, 1991, you proceeded to the site of the collision of two boats. With your aid, and the assistance of Mr. Kristopher Konkler, you rescued the injured boaters from a life threatening situation.

    Again, thank you for your commendable action and willingness to help others.

                              Sincerely,

                              P. J. McDONNELL, JR.
                              Lieutenant Colonel, EN
                              Acting Commander

Letter from Corps of Engineer for rescuing people in boat wreck

JAMES M. INHOFE
1ST DISTRICT
OKLAHOMA

PLEASE REPLY TO
☐ WASHINGTON OFFICE
ROOM 408
CANNON HOUSE OFFICE BUILDING
WASHINGTON, DC 20515
(202) 225-2211

☐ DISTRICT OFFICE
SUITE 305
201 WEST 5TH STREET
TULSA OK 74103
(918) 581-7111

PUBLIC WORKS AND TRANSPORTATIO
COMMITTEE

SUBCOMMITTEES
AVIATION
ECONOMIC DEVELOPMENT
PUBLIC BUILDINGS AND
GROUNDS
RANKING MEMBER

MERCHANT MARINE AND FISHERIES
COMMITTEE

SUBCOMMITTEE
COAST GUARD
AND NAVIGATION
MERCHANT MARINE

SELECT COMMITTEE ON NARCOTICS
ABUSE AND CONTROL

CONGRESSIONAL ARTS CAUCUS
EXECUTIVE COMMITTEE
CONGRESSIONAL TRAVEL AND
TOURISM CAUCUS
CONGRESSIONAL HUMAN RIGHTS CAUCUS
CO-CHAIR
AVIATION FORUM
Congressional Leaders United
for a Balanced Budget

Congress of the United States
House of Representatives
Washington, DC 20515

December 16, 1991

Mr. H. T. Konkler
2012 S. 123rd East Avenue
Tulsa, Oklahoma 74128

Dear Mr. Konkler:

Congratulations on receiving a "Lifesaving Award" from the U.S. Army Corps of Engineers for your efforts in rescuing eight people who were thrown into Fort Gibson Lake.

Your quick response to this emergency situation is truly worthy of recognition.

With best regards.

Sincerely,

JAMES M. INHOFE
Member of Congress

JMI/rb

Letter from Congressman Jim Inhofe for rescuing people in boat wreck

Kris and Heath fished a tournament on Grand in the snow. I pre-fished with Heath and we had over 20 pounds on our top five bass. Early that morning when Kris and Heath left for the ramp, there was snow in their boat. Kris and Heath managed to weigh-in 19 pounds and came in second place in the tournament. During the tournament, Heath called me and said when they were backing his boat into the water that one of the trailer running boards froze to the boat and came off. I got my tools, drove to the ramp and repaired his trailer while the boys were fishing.

In October 2009, we had a Tournament of Heroes on Grand. I volunteered to take out a veteran. His name was Russell Davis. We met at a gas station on Hwy 59 just south of Grove. We did okay, but did not win anything. There was plenty of fish to eat provided by those putting on the event.

That morning when I picked up Russell at the gas station, he said he just barely made it there because his vehicle was almost out of gas. Therefore, when

I took Russell back to his car I had him pull up to the gas pump and gladly paid to fill his gas tank. We should support our military every chance we get.

I love fishing and I think bass tournaments just add more excitement to catching fish. I love the competition, but I do not fish tournaments to make money. I fish to win and try to make enough money to defray the expenses of fishing. I fish hard with any of my partners, but I wear myself out when I am with one of my boys in a tournament.

When I was young, I would fish a day tournament in one bass club on one lake, drive to another lake and fish a night tournament in another bass club. It generally took me a couple of days to recoup.

In early days of fishing bass club tournaments, you not only won money, but also trophies or plaques. I have many of those trophies and plaques at our lakehouse on Grand. I had so many plaques stuffed in cardboard boxes that Trish finally convinced me to dispose of most of them.

20
Fishing in Old Mexico (1976 – 1986)

In the late 1970s and early 1980s, a group of us would go to Old Mexico and fish Lake Guerrero. The first trip to Guerrero was to Camp of the Big Bass on the north end of the lake. Bob Austin, George Hightower and I made the trip with other fishermen from Tulsa. Sometimes when we were in open water fishing mesquite trees in 30 feet of water we would be fishing with six poles at once. Each of us was fishing with two rods. One rod had a seven-inch worm on the

Tree where Bob caught 23 bass in a row in Old Mexico in 1976

George and Bob caught 4 bass on 2 cast in Old Mexico in 1976

bottom and one rod had a jig/grub hanging over the side about half the way to the bottom. There were times when we had five fish on at one time. Once when we were fishing in the flats with lots of trees, Bob caught 23 bass in a row under one tree fishing with a plastic worm. Another time Bob and George were throwing a Skipjack topwater and they caught four fish. Each had two on their topwater bait.

When we stayed at Chico's Camp, we fished areas we call the corral and the west bank. The corral was farmland that had a corral still standing under water. We caught as many as 100 bass in a day in that area. On the west bank, there were many mesquite trees in four to five feet of water. It seemed there was a three-pound bass in each tree. We fished a white spinnerbait between the "v" of the tree and you could call your shot; there would be a bass there. In the open areas on the west bank, we tossed Rattletraps and caught a lot of bass also.

Mike Toney hooked a small bass and while he was reeling the fish in, a big bass tried to eat the little one. It was a monster bass but Mike did not catch it.

Teddy Robinson got hung in a tree, so he trolled over to the tree and tried to get the lure loose. While he was leaning against the tree, he was pushing the boat away from him. He ended up hanging to the tree. He looked like a koala bear hanging on a tree with mid extremities in water. The water was cold. We had to go back to camp so Teddy could change his clothes.

We stayed at Chico's Camp, which was on the south end of the lake. Chico had a gas generator. We used it for lights and for electric knives to clean our fish. One of the guides in camp lived in a house made of beer cans.

Teddy, Chuck and Mike in Old Mexico in 1979

Teddy and I took our boys (Kris, Heath and Roger) to Old Mexico at Camp La Isla and one evening when we were fishing in the mid section of the lake in Corona River, we saw a big alligator. Next morning Roger was on the front deck of the boat and slipped off the deck into the water. He must have been thinking about that alligator because he

H.T. and Teddy in Old Mexico in 1980

Teddy, H.T. and Mike in Old Mexico in 1981

Teddy, Mike, and H.T. in Old Mexico in 1982

Mike and Teddy in Old Mexico in 1983

Matt and Dick in Old Mexico in 1984

Kris, Heath and Roger in Old Mexico in 1986

came up so fast and was in that boat before we barely knew he had slipped in.

When we stayed at La Isla Camp, we mostly fished the Corona River because that is where the big bass were found. There were some huge trees in the river. One time Teddy and I let the boys climb into a tree, and we took their picture.

This is where Heath got his nickname of Bubba. Teddy was called Bubba. He began to call Heath "Little Bubba." The nickname "Bubba" stuck with Heath. Family and friends still call him by that name today.

Heath was reeling in a salt craw plastic bait when we both saw a seven-pound bass swim up to the bait and grab it. Heath caught the fish. I caught a nice nine-pound bass and Teddy caught a bass that weighed over 12 pounds.

Kris and Roger in big tree in Old Mexico in 1986

Several times, we saw locals fishing for bass using nothing but a beer can with line wrapped around the can and a lure on the end of the line. They would cast the line off the can, wind the line on the can and jerk on the line if they got a bite. When they did catch a bass, they would just pull the line in with their hand.

H.T. with 9-lb bass caught in Old Mexico in 1986

Heath with 7-lb bass he caught in Old Mexico in 1986

Teddy with 12-lb bass he coutht in Old Mexico in 1987

21
Fishing in Canada (2000 and 2002)

Lake of the Woods in Canada and the USA is over 70 miles long and wide and contains more than 14,500 islands and 65,000 miles of shoreline.

In June of 2000, six of us, Larry Moffett, Richard Baker, John Cole, Ray and John Weaver and I made the trip to Lake of the Woods in Canada and stayed at Black Bear Camp. We caught largemouth and smallmouth bass, northern,

muskie and walleye. John caught the biggest fish, which was a long 50-inch muskie.

I told Kris, Heath, and Jeremy if they graduated from college that I would pay for a week trip on Lake of the Woods in Canada. Also for a Christmas present to Jimmy and Josh, I invited them on the trip. The six of us made the trip in May of 2002.

John and H.T. on Lake of the Woods in Canada in 2000

We loved fishing for northern pike with a spinnerbait in the weeds. They bit just like a largemouth bass. Once we got to catching a lot of yellow perch, so we decided to keep some of them to eat. Most people in northern states and Canada like to eat yellow perch as

Jim, H.T., Jeremy, Heath, Kris and Josh getting ready to go to Canada in 2002

much as walleye. We had about 30 in our livewell and when we were loading our boat onto the trailer, an elderly couple checked to see what we caught. They told us that is what they were trying to catch and really loved eating the yellow perch. We gave the 30 yellow perch to the elder couple.

Once Heath hooked a yellow perch and reeled it in when a big muskie grabbed the fish. Heath did a good job of playing the big fish on light tackle, but eventually lost the muskie when it spit out the yellow perch.

One night when we came back to camp, we noticed some fishermen were cleaning crappie. We did not even think about fishing for crappie at Lake of the Woods. They told us what part of the lake they were fishing. The next day we tried our luck and ended up catching a good mess of crappie to eat.

22
Fish Stories

In Eldorado, my favorite place to seine minnows, crawdads and perch for bait was in Sandy Creek. Another good place to seine minnows and crawdads was under a small bridge between Eldorado and the Duke cutoff road. The water under the bridge was knee deep and there was a hole after the bridge that was waist deep. In addition to the minnows and crawdads, we also caught small bass, perch and catfish, which were about the size of the minnows. Those fish were born in a pond upstream and when the pond overflowed, the baitfish would flow to the hole under the bridge. Once when walking to the hole we killed a big rattlesnake. Sometimes when seining for minnows, crawdads and perch we would catch a water snake in our seine. The last time I went to Eldorado, I noticed the hole was dry because of the drought in southwest Oklahoma the past few years.

Another place to seine bait was at the little creeks by the copper mine on the Elmer road east of Eldorado. The narrow creeks were easy to seine, but when we tried to seine the pits that were dug for copper, we would bog down in mud. The water was two feet deep and so was the mud, which made it very hard to pull that seine and walk in the mud.

Dad and I seined some minnows from Boggy Creek to use when we went to Lake Pauline in Texas for a cookout his work was having. We used a 10-foot seine because Boggy Creek was very narrow and it was easier to use than a 20-foot seine. We caught the minnows and when heading back to the truck, we saw a rattlesnake. We killed the snake and went on our way. I remember there was plenty of food and some of the men were rolling dice on a table. I took some of the minnows and fished for whatever would bite. I was a very tired boy when we left for home because I stayed up all night fishing.

When Melton was killed, I was working in Lebanon, OH selling Bibles for the Southwest Company. I took a day-off work that day and was on a river bank fishing for carp when some friends found me and told me the news. They took me to the airport and I flew to Wichita Falls, TX. Family members picked me up and brought me to Eldorado where Melton was buried.

I took my Champion Boat to Eldorado to fish Tom Steed Lake near Snyder, OK. I took both of my sons to the lake to fish for bass. While we were there, we talked with Jimmy Crumes, an Eldorado farmer, who was fishing for catfish out of his small aluminum boat. During the day, the wind got strong and Jimmy was going to have a rough time getting across lake to the boat ramp. I let him get in my bigger boat and we pulled his boat across the lake.

Trish and I visited her sister, Shirley, and brother-in-law, Gary, at Stillwater one weekend and we decided to fish a pond west of town. I bought some minnows. Trish would bait her own hook, but she would drop the minnow in the dirt first so she could handle it better before putting it on a hook.

When Trish and I lived in Oklahoma City, we took her niece, Tara, on vacation to Six Flags Over Texas. On the way there, we stopped at Lake Murray in Ardmore, OK. I rented an aluminum boat with a nine horse power motor and we went bass fishing.

Trish and Tara at Lake Murray

While we were there, Tara got into some of my medicine, so I gave her a spanking. I was not mad at her, but I was scared of what could have happened. I never wanted her to do that again.

I have given two spankings in my lifetime. One of those was to Tara and the other was to Kris. One day I came home from work, Trish said Kris had done something that deserved a spanking, so I gave him one. After the spanking, Trish asked me why I spanked him. I really think that those spankings hurt me more than Kris or Tara.

Trish, the boys and I went to a Tinsley reunion in Sedona, AZ. While there, we decided to go trout fishing in one of the lakes in the mountains. Melvyn Tinsley, my brother-in-law, took us to the lake, and we used whole kernel corn to catch the trout.

Trish and I took the boys on vacation in Arizona to visit her mother, Eula, and stepfather, Leon. Then we drove to California to visit with her brother, Melvyn, sister-in-law, Pattie, and son, Lee. On our way there, we stopped at a trout

Heath and Kris fishing for trout in Arizona

Kris, Lee, Heath, Trish, Eula, Melvyn and Pattie at Disneyland

farm to let the boys catch some trout. We had to keep every trout the boys caught, which turned out to be very expensive. Before I could get them to stop catching trout, my bill was over $20. At least they cleaned the fish for us and we got to take some fish to their grandfather and grandmother.

One time I took Trish, Kris, and Heath to Claremore to bass fish. Kris caught a drum that weighed about seven pounds and he wanted to clean it and eat it. I brought the drum home, cleaned it, cut it up in small pieces and cooked it. I do not remember how it tasted, but I am sure not the best fish I have eaten.

Trish liked to fish with me when it was not too hot or not too cold, so we would either go bass fishing at night or fish a jackpot

Kris with 7-lb drum caught at Lake Claremore

tournament from 8:00 P.M. to midnight. I loved those jackpot tournaments because we get to stop on the way home and eat an early breakfast. I do not know why, but it seemed those breakfast tasted the best. Trish got mad at me once when we had a shotgun start on a jackpot tournament on Tenkiller. I got her wet on takeoff and that did not set too well with her. We were in my Ranger boat with 145 HP Johnson Motor and the boat was named "Hot Chocolate."

Trish and I went to Hudson and put in at Bird Hollow. I wanted to teach her how to fish a plastic worm. I started fishing in Cabbage Hollow. I told Trish to watch how I tossed the worm by a stump and worked it back to the boat.

That very first cast I got a thump and I said, "Watch how hard I set the hook." I caught a two-pound bass. She tried her luck at worm fishing, but could not get a bass to take her bait.

The first bass Kris caught on a plastic worm was in Big Cabin Creek on Hudson. He was 10 years old. He caught the bass in the first cut on the left just past Highway 28 Bridge. The bass was 12

H.T. with bass by his boat named 'Hot Chocolate'

inches long, but he was excited about catching a bass on a worm. A few weeks later we were fishing the same lake but in Wolf Creek. I was fishing a spinnerbait and Kris picked up my 7-foot flipping rod with a gig/chunk tied on. He flipped the bait by a laydown log and caught a four-pound bass. I can still vision his hookset because I had told him to jerk hard if he got a bite. He almost pulled the fish out of the water on the hookset.

I took Kris, Heath, and George Brown to Eufaula and we put in at Eufaula Cove. We started fishing the riprap on the northwest side of Highway 69, north of the town Eufaula. We were throwing crankbaits and Kris got hung in the rocks. I got his rod, was pulling hard when the bait came flying toward us, and one of the treble hooks in the crankbait buried in Kris' arm. At the time, I did not know the proper way to remove a hook if one hooked himself. I took some snipers and tried to cut the hook so I could pull it out of his arm. Mistake, the hook buried more into his arm. Luckily, there was a hospital just a mile from where we were fishing and I took Kris to the emergency room. He got a shot and the doctor cut the hook out of his arm. You would think that ordeal would make Kris think about going home, but instead he was eager to go fishing again. As it turned out this was a great day to catch bass.

We went up the North Canadian River and fished in a cut about a mile northwest of Fountainhead Lodge. The bass were stacked in the cut. I would drift the boat against a stump on a point then they would cast either a crankbait or spinnerbait toward the bank. I did not even fish because Kris, Heath, and George were all catching fish. I just took the fish off the hooks and watched the fun. They caught over 20 bass on one point.

I had another bad experience with removing hooks from someone. Steve Biggers and I were fishing at Tenkiller. He was fishing with a Hellbender Crankbait when he got it stuck in his scalp. He was wearing a toboggan hat. I unscrewed the treble hook from the bait. It was buried in his scalp. Steve told me to use a filet knife that was in the boat to cut the hook out of his scalp. I did and we continued fishing after he took a couple of aspirin for a headache. I do not even remember what we caught that day other than Steve.

The proper way to remove a hook from someone is to use no-stretch fishing line, put the line in the bend of the hook, push down on the eye of the hook, then jerk the line away from the bend of the hook. If you go to this website… http://www.majorleaguefishing.com/video_list.aspx?pid=ebB7pJiRaKMEgFu XXut_8eMYlumNac5r&cat=0 you will see a video of how to remove a hook from your arm.

Several times when the boys were small, Trish would fix a picnic basket full of food and we would take the boys fishing. Sometime during the day, we would park the boat on shore and eat our lunch.

Trish and I took the boys sand bass fishing on Eufaula and took a picnic lunch with us. I put in at Belle Star and drove to open water outside of the cove. The wind was blowing but instead of heading back to Belle Star Ramp, I decided to go into a cove north of there and let the boys pick up shells on the bank. We ate lunch. While we were there, the wind got stronger. I decided to head back to the ramp at Belle Star. With the waves high, it was a rough ride. The boys were hanging onto my legs while they lay in the bottom of the boat and Trish was giving me the look of, "What in the world are we doing out here?" When we got to the ramp, while I was loading the boat, I stumped my big toe on a moss covered rock but did not think much about it. The next day I went fishing with Teddy Robinson and Bob Austin on Hudson. During that day, my leg began to hurt. I noticed a red streak going up my leg from the big toe. When we got home, I went to the doctor and he said gangrene was setting in. Luckily, he gave me medication to prevent any damage. The doctor told me the next time I stump my toe in water to do it in sterile water.

A group from Amoco went to Toledo Bend and my fishing partner was Walt Thomas. While we were there a tornado hit in our area. Walt and I were on the other side of the lake when the winds hit. We found a houseboat that was tied up offshore so we got on it to get out of the wind and rain. When we started back to the area where we were staying, we saw one boat tied to a tree and the angler was in the tree. Several trees were uprooted, but no major damage from the tornado hit our area.

We fished an area that looked like a pecan grove. The trees were in a row and it made good fishing. We caught a lot of bass by those trees. On the way home, a wheel bearing went out on my trailer. It was on a Sunday, but luckily, we found a store open that had a wheel bearing.

Whenever Grand is high either Grand River Dam Authority or Corp of Engineers will open the flood gates for a few days. Fish will come upstream to an area called 'The Blue Hole'. Many times, I took the boys to the hole. We caught a lot of catfish and some were big. One time Heath snagged a spoonbill weighing over 50 pounds and that caused a commotion. There were fishermen who lined the rock banks and that big fish had a lot of them scrambling to get out of the way of Heath landing his fish.

Speaking of spoonbill, below is a picture of the 96.75-pound spoonbill that John Bond caught on Grand and released alive on November 8, 2013. Following is John's account of the 'catch and release'.

W*e kept her at Jerry's house in a vat with oxygenated water from 8:00 p.m. Thursday night until 8:00 am. Friday morning. He got his front-end loader out and hooked it to a net under the fish to lift her up into the pickup. She was lowered into a 6-foot holding tank on the truck and we hauled her over to Grove Friday morning. She was weighed and certified right there on the corner of Main Street. Cars and trucks stopped, people came out of the stores, and teachers let kids leave the school grounds just to see the fish. The Daylight Donut shop owner five doors down even showed up to see what was going on. To say we had a crowd was an understatement. Sheila and Madaline (Jerry's wife) were there cheerleading as two big guys helped us get the fish on the scales.*

We returned the fish to the vat at Jerry's house and let her rest up for another five hours before releasing. Jerry got out his bigger front-end loader with a nine-foot bucket on the front of it, which he filled with water. Once we got her into the bucket with water, Jerry drove down his ramp and lowered the bucket into the lake and she swam out. She kept wanting to come to the shore. He said that was common of a lot of the catfish he had released over the years. We got the pontoon boat out and I laid down on the front deck and when we got close enough I grabbed her by the bill. Jerry put the boat in reverse and we towed her out into the lake about 200 yards into deep water. At that point with all of the water running through her mouth and gills she was really rejuvenated and ready to go. I turned loose and away she went. She was swimming well the last I saw of her.

My fifteen minutes of fame if you will. — *John*

Once some Amoco folks came to 'The Blue Hole' to try and catch some catfish. One was a top manager from Amoco. Heath was using shrimp dipped in Limburger cheese stink bait. When he tossed his bait into the water, he missed where he was throwing and hit the manager right in the back of his head. It did not hurt that much, but his hair did not smell too good. The

John with 96.75-lb spoonbill caught on Grand

manager was good-natured about it and made a comment that something like that could be expected while fishing around so many cat fishermen.

When I worked at Amoco, Dick Jones was my boss. He had a farm east of Tulsa near Inola. Dick had two ponds on his place and they were stocked with bass. He let the boys and I fish those ponds. I caught a lot of bass on different baits, such as spinnerbaits, buzzbait, jerkbait and jig/chunk. There was one laydown tree in one pond and I caught a six-pound bass out of that tree more than once. I used a jig/chunk and fished between a "v" in the tree limbs. That bass had a black spot on it so I knew it was the same bass. I caught a lot of bass in the three-to-five pounds range on buzzbait in those ponds.

Sometimes when I fished Grand, Hudson, or Fort Gibson and caught a lot of small bass I would bring them home, stop at Dick's ponds and stock the ponds. I also stocked the pond by the apartments on 21st street between Garnett and 101st street. I used this pond to test buzzbaits because it was close to where I lived in Tulsa.

I like a buzzbait that has a loud squeak because the noise seems to attract the bass. To get a squeak in the buzzbait I would tie it to a fan and let it run for hours, or hold a buzzbait out the window when I was driving a vehicle. I would turn the ear on a buzzbait so it would run left or right and put L or R on the bait. I would put a rod with the L bait on the left side of the front boat deck and a rod with the R bait on the right side of the front boat deck and then toss by boat docks on Grand. Best spots on docks to get bit were the corners or openings in the Styrofoam. I preferred the silver blade, but I had some made that had oxidized red, green, or gold blades. I put a plastic three-inch Mr. Twister grub or a four-inch Snaketrix as a trailer, and I always used a trailer hook. I liked a round piece of plastic on the main hook because it allowed the trailer hook to

swing.

Dick and I were fishing on Sardis and we were in Jack Fork South. We met an older couple, Fred and Jean Storer, from Tulsa who were trying to catch fish for a fish fry. After we

Postcard back and front of H.T. and Dick

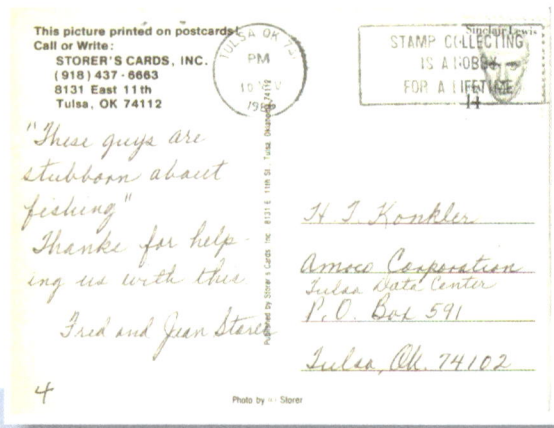

talked a bit, we found out they knew one of our coworkers, Todd Storer, who is Fred's brother. Fred asked if he could take a picture of Dick and I dressed in a skeleton mask. He wanted to make a postcard.

John Lorenzo and I fished Oologah many times when we worked at Amoco. Sometimes we would hook up the boat, head to the lake after work and fish until dark. John had an aquarium in his office and kept a small bass in it. John did feed the bass minnows. We watched that bass, trying to figure out what the bass was doing.

Jim Cleveland's folks had a place on Table Rock. When we worked at Amoco, we would take our families there and spend the weekend. At night, Jim and I fished the cove where his folks lived. I caught a six-pound bass in a rock pile by a boat dock with jig/chunk. I caught another six-pound bass on an extended point fishing a worm through a treetop, but those two did not compare to the eight-pound bass I caught the next day on buzzbait by a big tree. What was ironic was the BASSIN GALS were fishing a tournament that day and we were fishing in a cove where one of the teams was fishing when I caught the eight-pound bass.

When the boys were small, I took them on the navigation channel below Interstate 40. We launched near the small town of Webber Falls. I know the boys loved to fish because when I loaded the boat they were still fishing from the ramp. My favorite place was in Dirty Creek. I remember Jimmy Cleveland catching a big catfish on a buzzbait in the creek. Teddy Robinson and I had good catches on a yellow/black spinnerbait around stumps far up the creek.

H.T. with 8-lb bass caught on Table Rock

Homer Miller and Bob Austin had gone crappie fishing one Saturday on Hudson and were fishing in Cabbage Hollow. Homer and I had planned a fishing trip to the same place for Sunday. He told me that he caught a big spotted bass while fishing for crappie. We put on black jig/chunk and began fishing the bluffs just below Cabbage Hollow. Homer caught a big spotted bass. He jokingly told me if I would catch some fish, we would have a nice mess of fish. Luckily, I caught the next eight spotted bass. One of the spotted bass was 4.5 pounds and the biggest spotted bass I have ever caught. We ended up with 10 spotted bass and most were bigger than 2.5 pounds. I will never forget that fishing trip. The date was December 8, 1985.

I actually had fish jumping in the boat on Hudson. Cliff Stoops and I launched at Bird Hollow in the river and went to Cabbage Hollow to set out some limb lines for catfish. That night while driving the boat, but not on plane, shads were jumping behind the boat. Suddenly we heard a noise. I shone a flashlight inside the boat and a two-pound spotted bass had jumped into the boat. I guess it was trying to catch one of the jumping shad when it leaped into my boat. I thought, "The fish are jumping in the boat, so catching fish will be easy tonight." Wrong, we only caught one fish on our limb lines and that was a carp.

Guy Marney, the boys and I were fishing Eufaula in Duchess Creek area in my 'Hot Chocolate' Ranger Boat. I started to get on plane and head for the ramp at Porum when I hit something and spun the prop on my motor. I used the trolling motor to get back to the ramp. It was dark when we got there.

I was pre-fishing for a tournament on Hudson and I was up the river in a cut on the left. A boat was in the same cut. They were fishing a tournament. It was around 3:00 P.M. I talked with the men and they said they were weighing-in at Strang Bridge, so I planned to go watch the weigh-in. The boat left and

I was motoring out when I noticed something hit a shad by a laydown tree. I stopped the big motor, put down the trolling motor and made a cast to where I saw the fish hit the shad. I caught a six-pound bass. I made another cast and caught a four-pound bass. Back-to-back casts and I had two good fish. I went to the weigh-in and it only took 15 pounds to win. I was thinking, "Boy I wish I had fished the tournament because with other bass I caught, I could have won the tournament." My partner and I fished our tournament the next week, but I could not get those two big ones to bite.

A couple of times when I went fishing I saw deer jump into the water and swim across the cove. Once was when the boys and I were on Spavinaw fishing close to the spillway dam, we saw the deer jump in the water and began swimming to the other side which was a long way. We motored over and nudged the deer to get it to turn back to shore. The deer climbed out and ran off. The other time, I was with Dick Jones on Sardis and fishing in Jack Fork North Creek when we noticed two bucks swimming across the creek. They climbed out on the riprap, ran across the road and up the hill. I still do not know how they climbed through those riprap rocks without breaking a leg.

In 2001, Bo Conrad, an East Central High School classmate of Heath and Kris, told me his Uncle Homer Humphreys was fishing Fort Gibson in the Oklahoma Central Open BASS tournament. Homer called me and I told him if I was fishing the tournament I would fish Hickory Creek point, Sailboat bay area and around Toppers Ramp. Homer won the tournament on a small amount of weight. He was fishing around the docks by Toppers Ramp. I think that tournament was one of lowest weights (22.3 pounds) that a BASS tournament has had. At the weigh-in, BASS was selling merchandise so I bought a denim shirt with BASS embroidery on the shirt. I still have that shirt and wear it even though it is frayed and worn out. I have to keep it away from Trish because she thinks it looks terrible and wants to make rags out of it. Homer sent me some of his homemade spinnerbaits.

Larry Moffett and I went fishing on Hudson. We were fishing behind some islands up the river and using topwater. I caught a ten-pound carp on a jerkbait and Larry caught one the same size on a Zara Spook. To this day, I cannot explain why the carp hit the topwater baits.

Larry and I were fishing at night on Tenkiller and wore our insulated suits because it was cold that night. The next morning, we were fishing down a bank with our insulated suits on, and another angler was fishing the same bank in short sleeves.

Larry and I were fishing Skiatook and found a crappie swimming on top with a small perch lodged in its mouth. Larry picked up the crappie, removed the perch and both of them swam away.

Another time on Skiatook Larry caught a gar on a buzzbait. He asked me to grab the gar and get the bait out of its mouth. I did and my hands smelled terrible. It took a lot of soap to get that smell off.

Larry and I were fishing on Hudson in the back of Wolf Creek. Just as I went by a stump, I noticed a catfish was spawning in the middle of the stump. The catfish was about five pounds. I told Larry, "I think I can catch that catfish with my hands." I leaned over the gunnel, reached down and touched the catfish. It turned around and bit my hand. Larry got a big laugh. I got a sore hand.

Another time Larry and I were on Hudson and fishing up in Rock Creek close to the Highway 28 Bridge. I went a long way up the creek and we caught a few fish. When I started to leave, I got the boat on plane and ran the creek. Just after I passed the bridge, I made a wrong turn and ran onto a shallow mud flat. I could not move the boat with the motor or pushing with the paddle. We had to get out of the boat and push the boat off the flat. All the time we were doing that another fisherman was fishing nearby and he probably was thinking we were idiots. At least one of us was.

For a few years, we had the Largemouth Bass Virus and in most lakes, it only took 12 to 13 pounds to win a tournament. It was an anomaly to weigh-in a six- pound bass in a tournament when we had the virus. The virus only affected the big bass and they were dying, but there was one lake the virus had not affected, Hudson. Larry and I took his boat to Wolf Creek Ramp to put some new running boards on his boat trailer. After completing that task, we went up the lake and started flipping the willows. The lake was up two feet. Larry was tossing a big brush hog and I was tossing a jig/chunk. We caught a lot of fish in the three to six pounds range. I even managed to catch a couple of good ones on a chartreuse/white spinnerbait. This was in the middle of summer. We came back a week later and the lake was even higher. We did well again! In addition, we did a dog rescue, a dog we found in the middle of a tree. He was whining so we plucked the dog from the tree. We motored to the bank about 20 yards away and let the dog out on shore. He ran to a house that was a couple hundred yards away.

A group of us went to Lake Fork in Texas early in the year and it was very cold. Larry was with his father-in-law, Richard Baker, and I was riding with Tony Cordova in his 16-foot boat. We all had our insulated suits and motorcycle helmets on to protect our face when we were on plane. We motored up lake early one morning. By the time we got to our place to fish, I stood up and my insulated suit cracked because I had been sprayed with water and it froze on my suit. It was that cold. The good part is that Larry caught a 12-pound bass on a lizard. He put the bass in his livewell and weighed her at the place we were staying. Then Larry released her back into the lake. Larry also caught a seven- and eight-pound bass just before he caught the big one. We had a good trip fishing the plastic lizard and jerkbaits.

When we left Lake Fork, Larry and I drove to Sardis to fish a tournament. It was freezing and when we got there, the steering cables on Larry's boat were frozen. The motor would not move. Luckily, one of the guys fishing the tournament had an electric heat gun that we used to thaw the cables. We were not the only boat who had problems with steering cables freezing, so the electric heat gun proved a very handy tool.

Larry and I fished on the navigation channel east of Muskogee. We put in at 3-Forks Ramp and ran up river. We turned into a branch on the west side of the river and we were going slowly when we noticed a jeep that was upside down in the water. The first thing we did was to check and make sure no one was in the jeep. The tires were out of the water and looked new. Then we noticed the license plate. It had 'Bo Knows' on the license plate. Back then, the football player, Bo Jackson, had a commercial and in it, people would say 'Bo Knows'. On our way home from fishing, we stopped at the Highway Patrol Office and reported the vehicle in the water.

One of my favorite baits to throw in the early part of the year is a suspended jerkbait. Larry and I had a tournament on Grand, so I pre-fished on a Wednesday by myself. I caught 21 bass that day. Fourteen were non-keepers (buck bass) caught on secondary points. Seven were keepers between three and five pounds caught on main lake points in 25 to 30 feet of water. I was throwing a suspended jerkbait. Larry and I fished the tournament the next Saturday and weighed-in 22 pounds of bass fishing only main lake points. We won the tournament.

First bass caught on Alabama Rig by H.T.

Larry and I decided to go back on Sunday and our top five weighed 30 pounds. We had an eight, two sixes and two fives, and we caught other good fish. What a day on jerkbait. I could not stand it, so I took off work on Monday. I took Heath and his friend Jason Taylor and we had good catches again. In three days of fishing the jerkbait we caught 44 bass over three pounds each.

Now the bait that is competing with the jerkbait is the Alabama Rig or A-Rig. Anywhere that you catch fish on a jerkbait, you can catch them on an A-Rig. It is unbelievable the weight of five bass limits on the A-Rig. In some tournaments it was taking over 25 pounds to get a check.

My first two bass on an A-Rig were caught when fishing with Dave Patterson on Grand. The first one weighed five pounds thirteen ounces and the second one weighed five pounds and nine ounces.

For Kris' birthday one year, I hired a guide on Beaver Lake in Arkansas to try and catch striped bass. It was in March and the weather was cold. This is where I saw my first umbrella rig. It is the same as the A-rig, but it was not called A-rig back then. The bait was made with piano wire and it had five

Second bass caught on Alabama Rig by H.T.

big swimbaits. Jeremy and Heath went on the trip with us. Jeremy caught the biggest striped bass.

I participated three years in the Rush for Brush project on Grand that was sponsored by GRDA. Generally, about 100 volunteers would gather at the spillway or Martins Landing. We built artificial brush piles made from cinder

blocks with PVC tubing stuck in them and cemented in. They looked like a spider. The first year, 100 volunteers took home 12 brush piles each. The next year, I set out 15 brush piles and the last year, Rick went with me and we brought home 30 brush piles to set out. If you can find my boat dock, you will probably find one of those brush piles.

Jeremy and Kris with stripper Jeremy caught on Beaver

Jerry, my brother-in-law, knows quite a bit about Hudson because he and his uncle farmed the bottom land before the lake was filled. Jerry took me toward the pump back station, along a bluff, and showed me where an old roadbed ran and turned south going across a creek. He said an iron bridge is right here and sure enough, you could see the bridge on the locator. He then took me further out into the middle and showed me where there was a road intersection. Big trees lined the roads, which are now stumps. Then we headed to the dam. Jerry told

Kris and Rick unloading Rush For Brush piles made on Grand

me about a hump that was created when they were digging gravel and a road was built that spiraled up to the top. He said this was one of his favorite places to fish a worm for bass.

Dalton visited us in Tulsa once and we went to Hudson and fished Wolf Creek one afternoon. I was throwing a jig/chunk and caught two fish around six pounds and three or four more real nice bass. It was a good afternoon.

One of my favorite places to catch catfish was on ripraps on the lakes around Tulsa. I fished the riprap on Oologah, Keystone, Hudson, and Eufaula. The best time to fish the rocks was when the catfish were spawning. I would walk the riprap with a rod and reel with a slip cork set at two to three feet deep and baited with worms on the hook. When I saw a catfish roll on top I would toss the bait to the swirl and most times I would get a bite. If the catfish were not swirling on top, I would set out a couple of poles and wait for them to bite.

Pat and I went to Eufaula one early March day and went to a point where I lost a big smallmouth when I fished a tournament with Kris. We were throwing jerkbaits and Pat hooked a monster. We saw it once and it was bronze just like a smallmouth, but when we got it in the boat, it was a 10-pound buffalo. Pat

H.T. with 5-lb bass caught on Grand

and I had a great day fishing the jerkbait on riprap. We had a couple in the six pounds range, a couple in the five pounds range and several in the three to four pounds range. Pat hooked one that we did not see and he thought it was bigger than the six-pounder. Wish we had been fishing a tournament.

Rick and I like to fish Grand when the lake is up and in the willows. We were fishing in the back of a creek, I was throwing a chartreuse/white spinnerbait and he was tossing the sweet beaver in the black/blue color. In one cut I caught a six-pounder and two five-pounders. Then we ran to another cut and I caught another six-pounder. Then I tossed the spinnerbait by a willow tree and a big one broke my line. That was my fault for not retying often enough. Rick caught his fair share of big ones also. We were close to 30 pounds on five fish. The next day we went back to the same place and only caught a couple of three-pounders. The difference was that the sun was shining the day we did not catch them. Rick fished a tournament with Rodney Lowry a week later in the same area and they had 19+ pounds and received a nice check.

In August of 2004, Trish and I bought a place on Grand Lake. It is a three-bedroom house with fireplace, three-car garage and a two-slip boat dock. Our lake place has 240 feet lakefront property and goes 350 feet into the woods. We kept our Tulsa home.

Since Trish and I bought our lakehouse on Grand, I have caught more crappie in those 10 years than I did the past 60 years. What a pleasure it is to share the fun with family and friends! I believe crappie is the best eating fish and I eat my fair share of them. I have always loved catfish from the days of catching them on Sandy Creek and farm ponds in Eldorado, but crappie are hard to beat.

H.T. and Trish Lake House

Just this year I learned a better way to clean catfish. Jerry Kropff called me one day around noon at my lakehouse. He asked if I wanted to go and try to catch some catfish. He came by our place and picked me up. We went out and caught eight catfish between three and eight pounds, which by Jerry's standards are small catfish. He showed me how to remove the dark (stronger tasting) meat from the catfish filets. You end up with less meat, but Jerry says the answer to that problem is to catch more catfish.

Jerry held the catfish Grand Lake record (74 pounds on rod and reel) for a while and then the Oklahoma Department of Wildlife Conservation started new records with certified scales. Jerry held the record two or three more times, but current blue catfish record is 64.8 pounds caught by

Catfish that Jerry caught

Max Buzzard. Ironically, Max was in Jerry's boat using Jerry's catfish pole when he caught the fish. Jerry fishes catfish tournaments, generally with John Bond. They go to different states and do very well. Jerry is the best at catching catfish that I know and you are not going to beat him catching crappie either. He just knows how to catch fish. His love of catching catfish goes way back. His first date with his lovely wife, Madaline, was noodling catfish. Jerry said her dad was mad at him for keeping Madaline out all night on a date until he noticed the big catfish in the back of his pickup truck.

Every year in the spring or early summer Josh Tinsley, my nephew and Tyler Shelby (both are Oklahoma State Troopers) and Todd Abert would visit me at our lakehouse on Grand. I always looked forward to their visits. They usually stay three nights and I feed them rib-eye steaks, chicken wings and a fresh mess of crappie. They love breakfast composed of eggs, bacon or ham, biscuits and jelly. They set out limb lines and jugs for catfish, fish for crappie from the dock, and take my boat out if they want to catch bass or sand bass. If it is warm enough they will enjoy swimming from the dock. A friendly game of Texas HoldEm Poker is always fun to finish off the day. They always take home several quarts of catfish and crappie filets.

Tyler, Josh and Todd with catfish caught on Grand in 2012

Todd, Josh and Tyler with catfish caught on Grand in 2013

Josh, Tyler and Todd with catfish caught on Grand in 2013

23
My Favorite Lakes and Spots to Fish

Top Three Favorite Lakes:

Grand – Ketchum Cove, Duck Creek, Drowning Creek, Horse Creek, Honey Creek, Wolf Creek, Elk River, Neosho River.

Hudson – Wolf Creek, Spavinaw Creek, Rock Creek, Big Cabin Creek, and all the cuts on the river to the dam.

Eufaula – Duchess Creek, Brooken Cove, cuts on north bank from dam to Eufaula Cove, Fame Creek, Possum Creek, Longtown Creek, Gains Creek, and Coal Creek.

24
My Favorite Baits To Catch Fish

Favorite fishing bait for:

Bass – Spinnerbait, either yellow/black for muddy colored water or chartreuse/white for clear water.

Catfish – Limb lines and jugs with live perch or fishing a rod and reel on bottom with cut shad or perch.

Crappie – PowerPro braided 210 line (two pounds test in diameter, ten pounds test in strength), 1/16 ounce jig, generally with a red hook and a two-inch Gene Larew Bobby Garland lure in Monkey Milk (Shad) or Key Lime Pie (Chartreuse) color.

Perch – Pinch of nightcrawler on a very small hook.

25
Bass Pictures of Family and Friends

Kris with bass he caught on Grand

Stacie, Kris and Ainsley with bass caught on Grand

Stacie and Kris with bass she caught on Grand

Stacie with 5-lb bass she caught on Grand

Stacie with bass she caught on Grand

Kris with bass he caught on Grand

Kris with bass he caught on Grand

*Kris with bass he caught
on Grand*

*Kris and Heath weigh in
20.39 lbs in Nichols Tournment
on Grand*

*H.T. with bass caught
on Hudson*

Heath with bass he caught on farm pond

Heath with bass he caught on Eufaula

Sheila with 6-lb bass she caught and 4-lb bass John caught

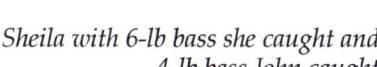

26
Catfish Pictures of Family and Friends

*Jeremy with catfish
he caught on Grand*

*Heath with catfish
he caught on Grand*

*Josh, Jim and Heath with catfish
caught on Grand*

*Heath and Jim with catfish
caught on Grand*

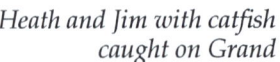

H.T. with catfish caught on Grand

Stacie and Kris with catfish caught on Grand

Ainsley, Stacie and Kris with catfish caught on Grand

Mark and Diane with catfish caught on Grand

Heath, Bo and JT with catfish caught on Grand

H.T. with catfish caught on Grand

Heath with catfish he caught on Grand

Kris, Ainsley, Stacie and Blake with catfish caught on Grand

Kris and Stacie with catfish caught on Grand

Kris and H.T. with catfish caught on Grand

H.T. with catfish caught on Grand

27
Crappie Pictures of Family and Friends

Rick and H.T. with crappie caught on Grand

Rick and Mike with crappie caught on Grand

Heath, Rick and Mike with crappie caught on Grand

H.T. with crappie
caught on Grand

Heath and H.T. with
crappie caught on Grand

Josh, Calton and Shelly with
crappie caught on Grand

Dave with crappie
he caught on Grand

H.T. with crappie caught on Grand

*Kris with crappie he
caught on Grand*

*Heath with crappie
he caught on Grand*

*H.T. with crappie
caught on Grand*

*Kris with crappie
he caught on Grand*

*Stacie and Kris with crappie
caught on Grand*

*Ainsley, Stacie and Kris with
crappie caught on Grand*

Kris with crappie he caught on Grand

Heath with crappie he caught on Grand

H.T. with crappie caught on Grand

H.T. with crappie caught on Grand

H.T. with crappie caught on Grand

*Rick with crappie
he caught on Grand*

*Dave, Larry and H.T.
with crappie caught
on Grand*

*H.T. with crappie
caught on Grand*

*Stephanie with crappie
she caught on Grand*

H.T. with crappie caught on Grand

Bo and Nic with crappie caught on Grand

Heath, Kris and H.T. with crappie caught on Grand

H.T. with crappie caught on Grand

Dave with crappie he caught on Grand

Bo and H.T. with crappie caught on Grand

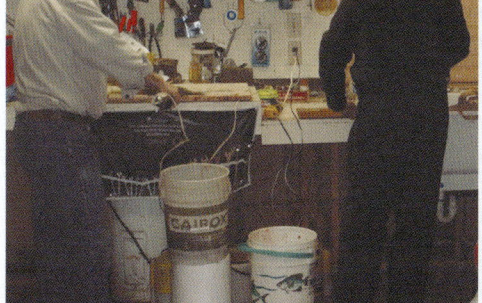

H.T. and Larry cleaning crappie

*Jeremy, Heath, Kris and Nic
with crappie caught on Grand*

*Kris with crappie
he caught on Grand*

*Kris and Bryan with
crappie caught on Grand*

*Kris, Nic, Stacie and Candi with
crappie caught on Grand*

*Larry with crappie
he caught on Grand*

*Larry with crappie he
caught on Grand*

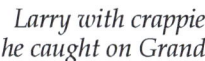

*Larry and Dave with
crappie caugh on Grand*

28
H.T. Konkler Fish Recipe

Crack open two eggs in a pan or bowl.

Add one cup of milk and stir.

Soak the filets in milk/egg mix.

Put wet filets on a plate or pie pan and salt and pepper both sides.

Fill a Ziploc bag with 60% flour and 40% cornmeal and mix together. For 10-12 filets, I would use 1.5 cups of flour and one cup of cornmeal. For 20 or more filets, I would use three cups of flour and two cups of cornmeal.

Put filets in the flour and cornmeal mix. I prefer a gallon size Ziploc bag to put the filets in. You can use any container but just make sure filets are covered well.

Place the filets in hot cooking oil. I use peanut oil, but any good cooking oil will do. I use a deep-fryer to cook the filets. The deep-fryer has a basket and I cook five to 10 filets at a time. If the oil is hot, it only takes about five to seven minutes for the filets to cook. They will float when done. If using a regular skillet, it will take a little longer for filets to cook.

When removing the filets from the oil, lightly salt the wet filet.

This recipe will work for bass, catfish, crappie and sand bass. If you are having a big fish fry and planning to use a lot of flour and oil, I suggest you make a trip to the Daylight Donut Flour Company at 11707 E. 11th Street in Tulsa. The flour is a special blend just for frying fish. You do not need to add cornmeal, and you can get good shortening to cook the fish. John and Sheila Bond own the company and are great people to work with.

29
Smith Family Reunion

Mom's maiden name is Smith and in October 2001 the Smith family started an annual reunion. Mom had five sisters and one brother. All are deceased except Aunt Lavern Wilson, the youngest in the family. She was 86 years old on December 19, 2013.

The first cousins are responsible for the reunions and we rotate the responsibility each year. Mom's brother, Lucian, was never married and had no children. Therefore, the siblings of Opal, Marie, Jewel, Mattie, Lavern, and Mom took responsibility. The first cousins would determine where we would meet, what the theme would be that year and what food would be prepared. We usually played games of 42 dominoes, bingo and 'Baggo'. For years, we picked partners to play 42 dominoes, but because Nova Hall and Mary Powell were so good and won the first two years, we decided to draw for partners. Below I have listed the dates of the reunion, where it was located, who was responsible, the theme of the reunion and what team won the 42 domino tournament.

Date	Location	Family Resp.	Theme	Winner of 42 Domino Game
10/6/01	Eldorado, OK	Lavern	Hawaii	No Tournament
10/5/02	Eldorado, OK	Lavern	Red, White & Blue	No Tournament
10/4/03	Eldorado, OK	Opal	Taste of Texas in Oklahoma	Nova Hall and Mary Beckett
10/9/04	Eldorado, OK	Marie	Texas Size of BBQ	Nova Hall and Mary Beckett
10/8/05	Eldorado, OK	Becky	Fin and Fowl	Nathan Rich and David Beckett
2006	*Skipped*			
10/6/07	Eldorado, OK	Mattie	Fiesta	Jerry Price and Harvey Willeby
10/4/08	Carlsbad, NM	Jewel	Italian	Nova Hall and Maxine Rich
10/10/09	Hempstead, TX	Opal	Real Texas BBQ	Nathan and Maxine Rich
10/9/10	Carlsbad, NM	Lavern	2010 Smith County Fair	Mary Beckett and Bob Donaldson
10/15/11	Carlsbad, NM	Marie	Fall Festival with Halloween Costumes	Joann Hopper and Judy Wilson
10/13/12	Eldorado, OK	Becky	Konkler Fish fry	Tommy Hopper and Maxine Rich
10/5/13	Willis, TX	Mattie	No Theme	Jap Hopper and Dalton Konkler

Smith Family Reunion in 2004

Smith Family Reunion in 2010

At our 2011 reunion, many wore Halloween costumes. Following were the awards:

- Best Costume – Aunt Lavern in her cat outfit – she was 83 years old
- Scariest Costume – Harvey in his Reaper with red eyes outfit
- Funniest Costume – Danny in his Howdy Doody make-up
- Sexiest Costume – Cody in his 'Where's Waldo' outfit
- Original Costume – H.T. in his fishing outfit with rod and reel and trophy

Aunt Lavern with her cat costume

*Danny with his
Howdy Doody makeup*

Harvey with his Reaper costume

*Cody with his
'Where's Waldo' costume*

My family was responsible for our 2005 Smith reunion. I sent out a letter asking each of my cousins, uncles and aunts to send me something that we might not know about them. Then I made a list, gave it out at the reunion and had everyone guess whose information it was about. Below are a few of them:

- In elementary school, I received an autographed picture from Bob Hope for a drawing I drew that looked like Mr. Hope. *(Mark Snow)*

- Over several years, we helped cook approximately 20,000 meals for teenagers at Christian Teen Summer Camps – all volunteer work. *(Ramona & O.C. Hollan)*

- I once kissed Bobby Sherman (teen idol in the late '60s, early '70s). He later wrote me two letters in his own handwriting. *(Shirley Price)*

- I was at the dedication of the new USS Arizona Battleship. I was also in the Navy and went on two Western Pacific cruises. *(Nathan Rich)*

- I was in Germany when the "wall" went down and I picked up a chunk of the wall. *(Harvey Willeby)*

- I had lunch with Mickey Mantel. *(Danny Wilson)*

- I attended the 1996 Olympics in Atlanta. *(Frank DeLaura)*

- We did not learn to ride a motorcycle until we were over fifty years old. We have traveled across the U.S. on one motorcycle. *(JoAnn & Jap Hopper)*

I have to mention a couple of quotes I got back from my uncles and aunt:

- Uncle Charlie had a son, Sonny, from a previous marriage and Aunt Jewel had a son, Harley, from a previous marriage, and both of them had Nathan. Quote from Uncle Charlie, "I used to tell my wife, you better go referee the boys because my son and your son are beating up on our son."

- My spouse asked me if I was going to the wedding of our daughter and I said, "I am not going to the wedding because I gave her away twice and she came back." (Uncle Bud)

- You might say I have been an operator. I was an elevator operator, a telephone operator, a school bus operator and a movie projector operator. (Aunt Lavern)

30
Little Things In Life Make A Big Difference To Me

Following are some examples:

Kris *(son)* –   Kris was in shop at school. He made me a walnut box to hold bottles of fishing bait called chunk, a long iron fork and tongs to use on the BBQ grill. I keep those articles at our lakehouse on Grand.

Jig and Chunk box holder Kris made for me in shop

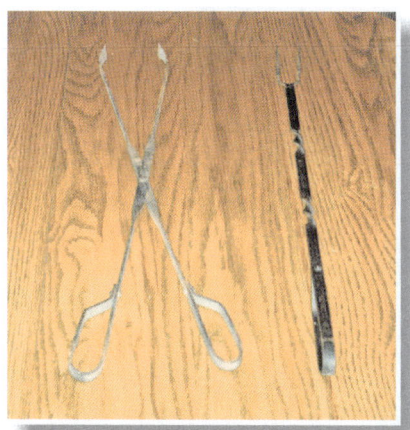

BBQ tongs and fork Kris made for me in shop

Heath *(son)* – Trish and I got a letter from one of his professors at OSU and after reading the letter it just made my day. I wrote the professor and told him that Trish and I appreciated the letter.

November 30, 1998

College of Business Administration
School of Accounting
401 Business Building
Stillwater, Oklahoma 74078-4017
405-744-5123
FAX 405-744-5180

Mr. and Mrs. H. T. Konkler
2012 S. 123 E. Ave.
Tulsa, OK 74128

Dear Mr. and Mrs. Konkler:

During this semester, I've had the opportunity to work with your son Heath in the written business communication course I teach in the College of Business Administration at Oklahoma State University. Having the opportunity to get acquainted with Heath has indeed been a pleasure. He has mastered well the important course concepts, enabling him to produce high-quality written work.

In addition to his academic ability, I've noticed a number of other personal characteristics that make Heath a pleasure with whom to associate. Heath works well with others, is respectful of their feelings, and enjoys being helpful. Furthermore, his pleasant personality earns quickly a high level of respect among those with whom he works. He is a mature individual who regularly displays good common sense. Many of his personal characteristics involve those values that were undoubtedly instilled in him at an early age. Your parental efforts are continuing to pay rich dividends; for that, I believe, you can be very proud.

Heath has played an important role in my having an enjoyable semester. I am indeed grateful for his presence in my class.

Best wishes for a wonderful holiday season

Sincerely yours,

Zane K. Quible
Professor

A wonderful letter from a professor at OSU about Heath

Rebekah *(granddaughter)* – When she was five years old (she is seven years old now), she made me a wooden cross with fishing line through it so I could wear it around my neck. It would not fit over my head, so I hung that cross on my 2007 Tahoe rearview mirror and every time I get into my vehicle, I think of her. Just this year I traded that Tahoe for another Tahoe, and when I went to put that cross on the mirror, I could not find it. I drove back to the dealership and searched the 2007 Tahoe, and found it where it had fallen between the seat and center console. It is now hanging on my 2014 Tahoe rearview mirror.

Hope and Rebekah

Rebekah

Rebekah playing softball

Hope and Rebekah getting ready to sing in church

Hope *(granddaughter)* – Once last year I went to Bentonville to watch Rebekah play softball. Hope and I were sitting outside at a table on their back patio. She was coloring in a book and I was just enjoying her company. She said, "Papaw, I love you." I said, "Hope, I love you too." Then she said, "Papaw you are special." That is a four year old talking!

Hank, Rebekah and Hope

Hope, Rebekah and Hank

Hope and Rebekah

Rebekah, Amber, Hope and
Heath hunting quail
with H.T.

Donna Konkler *(cousin)* - Trish and I had one babysitter for our two boys and that was Donna. We just did not want to leave our boys with anyone else. We trusted Donna and knew she would provide good care for our boys. We also knew if the boys did something wrong that she would not let them get away with it.

Donna

John

John Bond *(friend)* – In the middle of the night, John took me to the emergency room in his pajamas and stayed in the emergency room until he knew I was taken care of.

Rick Newman *(friend)* – I can honestly say Rick is my best friend. We have fished together for many years and spent many hours together at my lakehouse. He is the first to help clean out the septic tank, haul artificial brush piles, pull my boat to a ramp and helping with other things. He just does not say no to work and is always willing to help.

Rick

Judy

Judy Stroud *(friend)* - Judy is Trish's best friend. They shop and go to movies together. Judy also looks out for our place in Tulsa when Trish and I are gone. She picks up our daily newspaper and mail, and waters the plants inside the house.

I am fortunate to have friends like Larry, Dave, Guy, Chuck, Jerry, and many whom I call friend and it is just a pleasure to be around them. If I tried to list all my friends I would forget some, so I just listed a few who I fish and hunt with often.

31
My Financial Advisor

Before I retired, I wanted to find a financial advisor that I trusted. I wanted someone that would help Trish and I develop plans to manage our retirement funds and ensure those funds were secure. After talking with several financial advisors, I found that person and firm. It is Mike Mazzei, CFP, of Raymond James Financial Services, Inc.

Mike

When I retired, Trish and I decided to take a lump-sum retirement versus a monthly annuity. Then we rolled the lump sum into an Individual Retirement Account (IRA) with Raymond James Financial. I have complete confidence that Mike Mazzei and his staff have captured and documented Trish's and my personal and financial goals. They provide quarterly advice on those goals.

You have heard people talk about "Fifteen Minutes of Fame." My fifteen - actually eleven minutes of fame came when Mike and Raymond James Financial executives had a conference call and invited a customer to be on that call. I was the lone customer on that call. Raymond James Financial made a CD disk of that conference call and up to now uses that CD as a training tool at their different locations.

32
Medical History

Because of ulcers, in March 1969, I had a Hemigastrectomy and Vagotomy surgery (removed one-half of my stomach and nipped the vagus nerve that controls the flow of acid to my stomach). While in the hospital, I caught hepatitis. Since my enzyme studies would not get to normal, the Navy decided to discharge me from active duty.

Just two days before Thanksgiving in 1991, I had a heart attack. It was 6:00 A.M., just after I had taken a shower. Trish and the boys rushed me to the emergency room where they decided to keep me in the hospital for a while and do several tests. That morning I smoked my last cigarette. I had smoked them for 30 years. I missed six weeks of work, but I had no surgery.

On January 12, 1993, I had a quintuple bypass heart surgery. Since they removed a vein from my right leg to do the bypass, I now have a zipper from my chest to my right ankle. My surgeon, Dr. James Whiteneck, told me that if I did what he recommended for three months, I would be as good as new and could do whatever I thought I was big enough to do. Therefore, I fished 15 bass tournaments a year, went dove hunting in Eldorado in September and went pheasant hunting in South Dakota in November and quail hunting in Eldorado in November and December. That was in addition to my job and other activities.

Because I snored so much and sometimes at night, I would stop breathing and wake up choking really badly, I decided to have a test done to see if I had sleep apnea. I did and they had me started using a Continuous Positive Air Pressure (CPAP) machine in April 2004.

On June 8, 2005, I had an abdominal aortobifemoral bypass surgery. My legs were not getting enough blood through the arteries. My stomach was cut open and cuts were made in both groin areas to insert some Dacron tubing, about four inches of it. The surgery worked great for a year without any pain in my legs when I walked, but now I have the same problem. If I walk half a block, I get leg cramps, so I must stop for blood to circulate. The surgeon told me I could have an operation on the legs to get rid of the pain, but I would need surgery again in three years. I decided not to have surgery because there is no pain if I do not walk too far.

On December 3, 2007, I had arthroscopic surgery performed on my left shoulder.

On November 2, 2010, my cardiologist did an abdominal angiogram and determined I needed an angioplasty (balloon procedure) in one artery and a stent in another artery around the heart.

On August 21, 2013, I had a salivary gland stone removed from inside my mouth. A week later the cut started bleeding again and I had to go to the hospital to have four more stitches to stop the bleeding.

33
Basketball Official, Bowling And Other Happenings

I was a basketball official for several years and called some of the games that Wayman Tisdale participated in at Washington High School in Tulsa. Wayman was a three-time All American Gold Medal Olympian, former NBA star and world-renowned jazz musician.

Article about H.T being a basketball official:

Tulsa Torch

Tulsa, Oklahoma   March, 1979

Refereeing games provides exercise, fun for Konkler

Riddle: What wears black and white and refs all over?

Answer: H. T. Konkler

In his spare time, Konkler referees junior high and high school basketball games all around the metropolitan Tulsa area. He started his refereeing career five years ago. Since that time, he has officiated at hundreds of games.

Konkler makes a call as he referees a local junior high school basketball game.

"I started calling (officiating) games because I was getting bored in the winter months. I needed to get out and get some exercise," Konkler said. "And since I enjoy working with kids so much, this really appealed to me."

If keeping busy during the winter months was what he had in mind, he sure accomplished his goal.

"During the winter, it seems like I'm calling games just about

(Continued on next page)

H.T. officiating basketball

Article about H.T being a basketball official (continued from previous page):

every night. From Jan. 2 through Feb. 9 of this year, I called games on all but five week nights," Konkler said. "I also worked on three Saturdays. On one of those Saturdays, I called six games."

Konkler receives pay for his efforts, but said, "The money really doesn't amount to much once you've paid for your suits, shoes, and transportation. What makes it all worthwhile to me is the excitement and the exercise. It's a lot of fun and really gets my adrenalin pumping."

Refereeing must, however, have its disadvantages. How about the hassling officials always seem to receive from players and fans.

"That sort of thing doesn't bother me one bit," Konkler said. "I'm just too easy-going to let something like that get to me."

Konkler, who is a member of the Oklahoma Secondary Schools Officials Association and the Greater Tulsa Officials Association, said he intends to continue

H. T. Konkler

"calling" games, but has no specific goals about advancing on to the college or professional ranks.

"The junior high and high school games are all I am interested in right now," he said. "I just plan to continue what I'm doing. I really enjoy it."

While working for Amoco I bowled on many teams. My favorite time bowling was with a coworker, Joe West. Joe and I bowled in a mixed league with Linda Smith and Debbie Scherer. We were average bowlers and won our fair share of games. I always enjoy Joe's Christmas letter about his family especially those beautiful granddaughters.

Joe

On August 10, 2004, Trish and I bought our lakehouse on Grand. Jack and Ruby Bickhard were our neighbors and what a blessing to have them as neighbors. They were 80 years old in 2004 and I quickly found out that they were in much better shape than me. Each day they walked to our mailboxes, which is a

mile up a steep hill. Neither Jack nor Ruby fished much, but I was welcome to fish on their dock anytime. Whenever I cleaned crappie, I would generally take a quart of crappie filets to them. On special events, for example, their birthday or anniversary, I would invite them over to enjoy a meal of crappie, baked potato and baked beans. Jack passed away on February 12, 2013, and we lost a true patriot.

Jack and Ruby

Jack, Ruby, Jean and Wayne eating some crappie

In 2005, I was a Board of Director at Red Crown Credit Union. I volunteered for one year only because I knew I was retiring in 2006 and I wanted to be sure not too many things interfered with my time at our lakehouse on Grand.

On March 12, 2006, **Rebekah Faith Konkler** was born, the daughter of Heath and Amber, and our first grandbaby.

On March 31, 2006, I retired from IBM with 33 years and 9 months of service (this service included Amoco, BP, PwC and IBM).

Rebekah

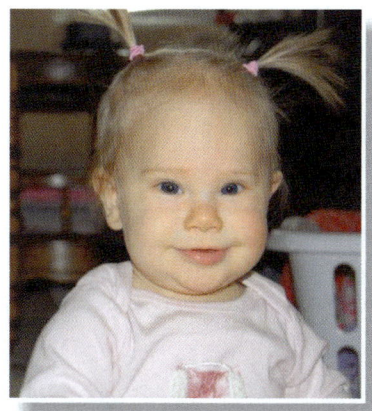

Hope

On July 15, 2008, **Hope Alison Konkler** was born, the daughter of Heath and Amber, and our second grandbaby.

Hank and Trish

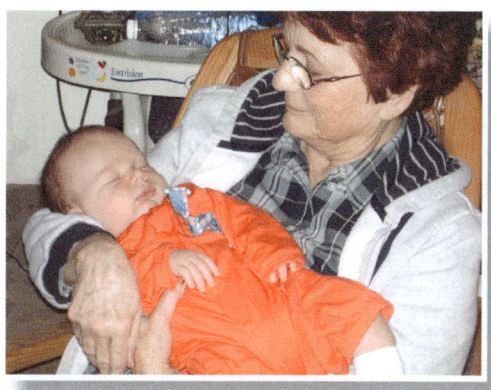

On December 7, 2012, **Hank Titus Konkler** was born, the son of Heath and Amber, and our third grandbaby.

I have six people who I regularly email, and guess what, they are all women. Their names are:

Ramona Hollan – *First cousin*. Ramona is 12 years older than me and growing up we did not get to visit much. When we started having our annual Smith Family Reunion in 2001, we started emailing each other and became great

pen pals. She is the proofreader of this book.

Diane Snow – *First cousin.* Another cousin that became great pen pals via email. We call each other 'Cuz'. Diane, Mark, and Stephen have been to our lakehouse and we always have fun and eat well.

Ramona, Dena, Tanna and Taiden

Steven, Mark and Diane

Jap and Jo Ann

Jo Ann Hopper – *First cousin,* actually a double cousin. Dad married Mom, and Dad's brother, Johnny, married Mom's sister, Mattie. When I went through Navy boot camp in San Diego, Jo Ann and Jap lived there. They picked me up at the Navy base and cooked me a great dinner. They now live in Texas. Jo Ann and Jap have been to our lakehouse and they plan to return to catch some of those crappie.

Priss Vanover – *First cousin.* Her name is Dorissa, but we have always called her 'Prissy' or 'Priss'. She is a great pen pal and keeps me up-to-date on her family. Her husband, Jeff, is retired and makes benches. He made me one for Rebekah and one for Hope. Rebekah's bench is at our lakehouse and Hope's bench is in the girls' room in Bentonville.

Priss

Pattie Tinsley – *Sister-in-law.* Pattie and I keep each other updated on our latest fish catches. She lives on Martinez Lake in Arizona. She has been to our lakehouse and is planning another visit.

Pattie with crappie caught on Grand

Pattie with bass caught on Martinez

Pattie with trout caught in the mountains

Pattie with catfish caught on Martinez

Shirley Huckabay – *Sister-in-law.* She says I am her favorite 'fav' brother-in-law. Actually, I am her only brother-in-law. Shirley and Trish spend half the year each in Eldorado taking care of their mother. They are special. Shirley has been to our lakehouse.

Shirley, Josh and Trish

Shirley

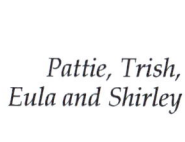

Pattie, Trish, Eula and Shirley

Trish

When Trish was young and lived in Texas, they had a potbelly stove to keep their house warm. She would warm her hands, put them to her face, then go to Eula and look like she is sick. Eula would feel her face and say, "I think you have a fever, maybe you should not go to school today." Shirley knew what Trish was doing and she would mock Trish. We, too, had a potbelly stove when I was young. At night I would back up to it and get warm then go jump into bed between those cold sheets.

After I started to work for Amoco, I began to write poems to Trish on Valentine's Day, her birthday and our anniversary. Because I wrote so many poems about her, I sometimes had to review previous poems to make sure I did not write the same thing.

Favorite Quote: Trish asked me what I was doing tomorrow. I said, "Nothing." She said, "You did that today." I told her, "I was not finished."

*From Sandy Creek to
Major League Fishing™*

34
Boat Official For Major League Fishing™

To learn more about Major League Fishing (MLF) go to *www.majorleaguefishing.com.* I am a Boat Official for MLF. The role of a Boat Official is to:

- Accompany an Angler throughout each day's competition.

- Weigh and record the weight of each scorable (generally 12 inches in length) bass into an iPad, which updates the real-time leaderboard.

- Notify Angler whenever the leaderboard changes.

- Enforce the rules.

- Assess penalty violation "on the spot".

- Perform assignments given by MLF staff.

Mitch, John, Martin and Larry

Larry, Randy, John, Greg, Dan and H.T.

Larry Coulson: Retired Fireman
Randy Fowler: Mechanical Tech for Gas Transmission Company
John Bond: Owner of Daylight Donuts Flour Company
Greg Koch: Wildlife Consultant
Dan Hayes: President of Oklahoma Custom Canvas Products, Inc.

Starting this year 2014, the MLF Commissioner, Don Rucks, asked me to be his assistant with the following additional responsibilities:

H.T.

- Evaluate and rate each member of the current Boat Official Staff and make recommendations to the Commissioner.

- Evaluate all Boat Official duties, procedures and communications, and make recommendations to the Commissioner.

- Serve as the on-site liaison between the Boat Officials and the Commissioner.

- Serve as the on-site liaison between the Boat Officials and Happy regarding boat repairs.

- Serve as the on-site liaison between the Boat Officials and the Anglers as required.

The inaugural MLF event was on Lake Amistad near Del Rio, TX in November of 2011. It was televised on Outdoor Channel in April of 2012. Each event consists of six days of tournament competition by 24 of the world's best bass anglers. Day one I was in the boat with Mark Davis, second day with Todd Faircloth, third day with Kelly Jordan, and the last three days I was a chase boat for Mike Iaconelli, Alton Jones, and Brent Ehrler. The Champion of this event was Brent Ehrler.

The next event was on Lake Chautauqua near Jamestown, NY in August 2012. It was aired on Outdoor Channel in January of 2013 and final day of tournament was aired on NBC on Feb 9, 2013. Day one I was in the boat with Gary Klein, second day with Skeet Reese, third day with Jason Quinn, and the last three days I worked with Edwin Evers, Dean Rojas, Mike McClelland, Bobby Lane, and Jason Quinn filming commercials. The Champion of this event was Denny Brauer.

H.T. and Brent

Kelly and H.T.

H.T. and Gary

H.T. and Todd

The day I was with Skeet, while he was dropping me off at the ramp, the wind was blowing hard behind us. I was on the bow of the boat and the cameraman was between Skeet and me. I stepped up to the dock with one foot on the dock and when Skeet put the boat in reverse, I fell hitting my knee on the dock. I was in the water up to my waist with an iPhone on my belt. People were running to me and asking if I was hurt. I said, "Yea, my pride is hurt." I just walked out on the ramp to my Tahoe and got in the vehicle soaking wet. Did my iPhone work? – No. Someone told me to put it in rice, so I went to the store and bought some Uncle Ben's Rice. I poured out half of it, put my iPhone in the box and poured the rice back in the box. After the iPhone was in the rice for 24 hours, I charged it and it worked, and still is working today.

The second event of 2012 was in October on Lake Istokpoga in Lake Placid, FL and was aired on Outdoor Channel in April 2013. Day one I was in the boat with Tommy Biffle, second day with Edwin Evers, third day with Gary Klein, fourth day with Brent Ehler, fifth day with Florida Wildlife Officials and Kelly Jordan shocking fish in zones already fished. The last day I worked with a photographer shooting still photos of the Anglers. The last day turned out to be quite a chore because we were getting some of the effects of hurricane Sandy. The Champion of this event was Edwin Evers.

Edwin and H.T.

Mike and H.T.

Tommy and H.T.

The first event of 2013 was in August on multiple lakes around Alpena, MI and was aired on Outdoor Channel in January 2014. Day one I was in the boat with Shaw Grigsby, second day with Dean Rojas, third day with Byron Velvick, and fourth day we did some still photography in a boat with Mark Davis and Gary Klein. The fourth day, which was a Thursday, was quite an ordeal for me because I had to make a trip to the emergency room.

H.T. and Byron

H.T. and Kevin

It was Wednesday, August 21, before we left on Friday, that I had a salivary gland stone (about the size of a black-eyed pea) removed from inside my mouth and two stitches put inside my cheek. The stitches were to dissolve in about a week.

Thursday, August 29, just before midnight, I woke up with a mouth full of blood, which I spit into my sink. I tried to get the bleeding stopped by pressing a towel against the cut. When I could not get it stopped, I called John Bond, another Boat Official, who was rooming next door to me at the hotel. I met him at his door and I messed up his sink with lots of blood. John quickly rushed me to the hospital emergency room. He was in his pajamas and did not give it a second thought about staying at the emergency room until he knew I was going to be taken care of. I was taken to the operating room around 2:00 A.M. The surgeon told John I would be there overnight and probably released the next day. John gave his phone number to the hospital folks to call him if I needed assistance.

The next day when the nurse came into my room and asked me if John Bond was my next of kin, I said, "No, just a true friend." John also contacted the cleaning personnel at the hotel. He told them why the blood was in our sinks and they probably needed special cleaning. My sink was spotless when I returned to my room at noon Friday. By the way, the operation involved putting me to sleep and putting four new dissolvable stitches inside my cheek. I met John in November 2011 at our Amistad event. I believe he is one of the most dependable, organized, hardworking and trustworthy individuals I ever met.

H.T. and Randy

Jeff and H.T.

35
And Finally

Finally, let me sum up my life and values. I love to fish and hunt, as you can tell from the above documented pages. I love God and family, and I enjoy my friends. I have great respect for those who have good moral values. I try to keep my promises. I focus on other people, not myself. I try to see the world the way it is, not the way I want it to be, and I always try to make fact-based decisions.

It seems the older I get, the less I remember, especially names of people. When I told Larry I was writing a book about my life, he said, "Did you not tell me you have CRS disease?" CRS stands for 'Cannot Remember Stuff' or something like that. I told Larry that I would be talking to someone about my best friend and I will say, "My very best friend, oh, what's his name?"

All the fishing and hunting stories did not come to me all at one time. I would think of something in the middle of the night and I knew if I did not get out of bed and write down my trend of thought that I probably would not remember the next morning, so a lot of the above stories were captured between midnight and early morning.

I am a simple man who believes anything is possible if you work hard and apply yourself. I am at the point in my life where "I don't sweat the small stuff anymore." I am involved with what interests me (emphasis is on interests). I try to pass on what I have learned in life. To me the best things in life are not things, and I am not young enough to know everything.